Journeys of the Spirit

Other titles in the Toolkit Series of books, developed and published by the Ministries and Faith Development staff group of the Unitarian Universalist Association of Congregations:

Nurturing Children and Youth: A Developmental Guidebook
by Tracey L. Hurd

Stirring the Nation's Heart: Eighteen Stories of Prophetic Unitarians and Universalists of the Nineteenth Century
by Polly Peterson

Stories in Faith: Exploring Our Unitarian Universalist Principles and Sources Through Wisdom Tales
by Gail Forsyth-Vail

When Youth Lead: A Guide to Intergenerational Social Justice Ministry, Plus 101 Youth Projects
by Jill M. Schwendeman

Journeys of the Spirit

Planning and Leading Mission Trips with Youth

Jennifer McAdoo and Anne Principe

Jessica York and Judith Frediani
Developmental Editors

UNITARIAN UNIVERSALIST ASSOCIATION

BOSTON

Printed in the United States

ISBN 1-55896-572-6
978-1-55896-572-0

14 13 12 11 10
5 4 3 2 1

Library of Congress Cataloging-in-Publication Data

McAdoo, Jennifer, 1960-
Journeys of the spirit : planning and leading mission trips with youth / Jennifer McAdoo and Anne Principe ; Jessica York and Judith Frediani, developmental editors.
p. cm.
Includes bibliographical references and index.
ISBN-13: 978-1-55896-572-0 (pbk. : alk. paper)
ISBN-10: 1-55896-572-6 (pbk. : alk. paper)
1. Church group work with youth—Unitarian Universalist Association. 2. Unitarian Universalist Association—Education. 3. Youth in missionary work. 4. Short-term missions. 5. Service learning. I. Principe, Anne, 1962- II. York, Jessica, 1962- III. Frediani, Judith. IV. Title.
BX9856.M32 2010
259'.23088289132--dc22
2010028693

To all those who see dandelions in their field of dreams.

—A. P.

To my family y a los niños, a sus familias y al personal en Camino Seguro.

—J. M.

Contents

Foreword

This how-to manual by Jennifer McAdoo and Anne Principe is terribly important. It is about what the Unitarian Universalist Service Committee (UUSC) refers to as "experiential education." Such experiences go by many names, but in essence they are about the growth of individuals and groups who leave their comfort zone and go elsewhere to encounter people or situations that are perceived as "other" or "different." Sometimes the journey is to a foreign country, sometimes to a distant corner of our own country or state, or simply across town or to another neighborhood. Whatever the destination, whomever you encounter, with whomever you travel—all can be adventures of the spirit.

"Others" may make us uncomfortable because we don't know them, we have stereotypes about them, or we don't know what to expect from them or what they will expect from us. They may have different economic circumstances, be of another race, or speak a different language. They may be people who seem quite like us, but are strangers. Even as participants, we may not know each other very well, and so may be part of "the other." Or the "different" may be that we are doing something we have never done before or going someplace we have never been before.

For more than twenty years, the UUSC has offered a variety of experiential educational opportunities. Because experiential education at the Service Committee is about social justice and human rights, in some ways such encounters always involve several fundamental tenets of Unitarian Universalism: the inherent dignity and worth of every person; justice, equity, and compassion in human relations; and the goal of world community with peace, liberty, and justice for all. Such an adventure could also be about nature, in which case it might involve respect for the interdependent web of all existence. In almost all cases, the experience will engage—and perhaps challenge—our values, as well as the values of people we encounter.

Such encounters hold great potential for fun and personal growth. On the flip side, they can feel challenging and leave participants confused, angry, or upset. Part of the purpose of this manual is to prevent frustration due to improper planning. However, often participants will experience negative emotions when confronted with injustice in our world. This is normal, and a thoughtfully guided experience should help youth and adults alike explore such feelings and learn how to use the accompanying energy to create change.

Spiritual adventures should be about crossing boundaries of some type. Some boundaries are more difficult than others. For people of privilege, crossing class boundaries can be quite complex. The Latin American writer Eduardo Galeano speaks eloquently of vertical versus horizontal relationships. *Vertical* means an encounter in which one has power, wealth, or status and reaches *down* to another, often involving charity or pity. *Horizontal* means that while such differences may exist, people reach *across* to one another to meet in solidarity, recognizing one another's inherent dignity and worth.

There should be some discomfort in a spiritual adventure; without it there is almost never growth. If we don't deny discomfort, if we explore it gently and respectfully while striving to understand it, discomfort can become a source of wisdom.

On the UUSC's JustJourneys and JustWorks experiential learning trips, we have had members of Congress, ministers, congregation members, and youth and young adult participants tell us, "It has been one of the most powerful and memorable experiences of my life." Others have been less enthusiastic.

What makes the difference between a powerful or disappointing adventure of the spirit? In my experience, the difference can be about thorough planning, good leadership, reflections that include open and frequent communication between participants and staff, shared expectations, a nonjudgmental attitude, and flexibility on the part of both participants and staff. These necessary elements are like fingers of a busy hand that need to be continually aware of each other and working together. There will always be unknowns that cannot be controlled; that's the way life is. However, planning, leadership, and communication are the fingers that ensure the invisible hand holding the participants throughout the spiritual adventure is welcoming, supportive, protective, and—when need be—firm.

Whether you are a seasoned trip leader or someone new on the block, this manual is full of reminders that can help ensure your congregation's spiritual adventure is emotionally meaningful, physically safe, and fun. We have repeatedly found that an unexpected product of the spiritual adventure is the deepening of relationships among participants, an enduring gift to these individuals as well as their congregation. Another frequent gift is growth in participants' Unitarian Universalist identity.

Sometimes the French say "courage" when departing and sometimes "bon voyage." We wish you both.

Charlie Clements is the former president and CEO of the Unitarian Universalist Service Committee.

Preface

Imagine you are crossing the threshold of a Unitarian Universalist congregation for the first time. You open a copy of the hymnbook, *Singing the Living Tradition,* turn to page two, and look at the seven Principles that Unitarian Universalist congregations affirm and promote. As you read phrases like "inherent worth and dignity," "justice, equity, and compassion," "world community," and "peace, liberty, and justice for all," you sense that the UU religious tradition is committed to the well-being of others.

You notice that our living tradition draws from many Sources, including "words and deeds of prophetic women and men which challenge us to confront powers and structures of evil with justice, compassion, and the transforming power of love." But it might take you a bit longer to uncover just how vast and deep our history of service to the wider community runs. Our legacy, according to Rev. Richard Gilbert, calls Unitarian Universalists to a prophetic imperative—a religious mandate to address the systemic problems of society. Given the complexities of today's world, social change cannot depend on a few charismatic individuals, but calls for the combined energies of those joined together for the common good.

As a religious tradition, Unitarian Universalism has a reputation of living out the call to social justice. Its concern for the wider world is part of the fabric—the curriculum, if you will—of the work we do in our congregations. That we may respond to the prophetic imperative, Gilbert challenges our congregations to "grow people of prophetic fire who will understand that helping to repair the world is no extracurricular activity, it is simply part of what it is to be Unitarian Universalist."

That challenge has been fundamental to our work as religious educators. Together we have more than fifteen years of experience serving four Unitarian Universalist congregations, where we have been charged with nurturing the spiritual growth and development of children and youth—from preschoolers to high schoolers—their parents, and the other adults who lead their classes and facilitate their youth groups.

Our experience tells us we must work intentionally to grow people of prophetic fire. We must give our children age- and developmentally appropriate opportunities to understand the complexities of the world we live in and to make a difference. A mission trip provides a curriculum to achieve these goals that is especially well suited for the age and developmental needs of youth. Planning, undertaking, and debriefing a mission trip offers rich opportunities for leaders and participants to educate themselves about oppression, bear witness to oppression, and share their privilege and good fortune by doing the work to help dismantle and overcome oppression.

Mission trips capture the passion and imagination of youth. They require youth to meet high expectations; face rigorous physical, emotional, and spiritual challenges; make preparations that can be painstaking at times; and live in community according to a covenant. We have witnessed youth who have responded deeply to the transforming power of love. Within the trajectory of lifespan faith development, a well-planned mission trip offers youth unparalleled ways to find meaning and direction in their lives.

We have written this book to help Unitarian Universalist religious educators, lay adult leaders, and youth leaders understand and undertake mission work with youth. It is both a practical manual for planning each step of a mission trip and a guide to creating and supporting the spiritual transformation of mission work. We share our philosophy of mission work and practical information on the mechanics of launching a trip, including spiritual preparation and ways to facilitate personal reflection. We hope to help readers anticipate with confidence and openness the unexpected, the mystery that is part of any sacred journey.

People who sign up for mission trips often have an altruistic desire to help others as a way to help transform the world. Rarely do they, themselves, expect to be transformed in the process. Discomfited? Yes. Challenged? Sure. But transformed?

Transformation is at the heart of any mission trip. We leave our comfort zones to travel into unpredictable situations. We make an outward journey, experiencing new places and new circumstances with a group of people we might not know very well. In doing so, we also experience an inward journey, equally unpredictable, equally full of mystery and wonder. As we open our hearts to our new surroundings, make ourselves vulnerable to the unknown, and allow ourselves to love and to be loved, we change—and it is through our *own* transformation that we transform the world.

We hope the challenges of doing a mission trip and the possibilities it offers excite you, and that you find this handbook useful as you plan your trip and set off for places near or far. Most of all, we encourage you to remain open to the mystery that awaits you on this sacred journey.

ONE

Introduction

> No journey carries one far unless, as it extends into the world around us, it goes an equal distance into the world within.
>
> —LILLIAN SMITH

An understanding of our concept of a mission trip begins with the meaning of the term *mission.* Among its many definitions of the word, *The American Heritage Dictionary* includes "a body of persons sent to a foreign land by a religious organization . . . to spread its faith or provide educational, medical, and other assistance" and "an organization for carrying on missionary work in a territory." For the purposes of this guidebook, we define mission as an inner calling to pursue an activity or perform a service—a vocation.

In his article "What Is the Mission of Missions?" (*Clergy Journal*, September 2006), Rev. Dan Hotchkiss, senior consultant at the Alban Institute, says a mission is a social ministry that helps others and changes the lives of its own members. A mission trip with youth is a unique opportunity to experience and expand notions of what it means to live in community, guided by our Unitarian Universalist Principles.

It is common for participants initially to be uncomfortable calling a justice-based trip a "mission trip." Given the implications of this term, the group needs a unified vision of purpose. Too many various goals—for example, to take a spiritual journey, to do community service, and to travel together—can compromise the integrity of the vision. A clear purpose, grounded in spiritual and faith development, is the defining element of a mission trip.

Well-planned, intentional justice work guides, shapes, and makes real lifelong commitments to social justice for youth. Youth create and cement relationships in a context unlike other social venues. Working directly to understand and help people who live in an environment or situation where resources to meet basic needs are inadequate can be a powerful experience. Mission trips grounded in Unitarian Universalism can transform our Principles from an abstract list to deep understandings based on a hands-on experience that will connect with the learning styles of many youth.

This guidebook is in your hands presumably because you believe a youth mission trip may be worthwhile for your group. The world of possibilities for youth programming is vast, and a mission trip is a major undertaking. For this reason, we highlight some of the benefits. A mission trip can

- present opportunities for intense community building
- maximize multigenerational time together
- engage the entire congregation on many levels
- develop youth and adult leadership
- deepen faith identity
- provide powerful transformational and spiritual experiences
- invite a direct relationship between participants and people in need.

This guidebook addresses the elements, both basic and complex, that comprise a youth mission trip. We assume that leadership includes a combination of religious professionals, lay adults, and youth. You will find guidance and a framework here to help lead a group through planning and preparing for its mission, traveling together, and continuing the work after returning home. The combination of philosophical, theological, faith development, and practical advice will help leaders shape a safe, meaningful, and transformative mission trip.

How to Use This Book

This guidebook will take you from planning the practical issues of a mission trip to reflecting on your own spiritual and faith formation. It will show you how to guide group processes that prompt participants' actions and nurture their meaning-making.

These pages contain an organizational framework for coordinating a congregational mission or service trip. The information is arranged sequentially. If you or your group are new to this work, you will find information to help you get started. We identify considerations for planning the logistics of the trip. In Chapter 8, five testimonials demonstrate a mission trip's potential to transform youth into people committed to transforming the world. We provide a Resources section loaded with research and planning checklists, information sheets, templates for planning sessions and worship gatherings, and other tools to help you along the way. Tailor the information and resources to fit the needs of your group. Be creative in your implementation.

A mission trip provides great opportunities for learning—even for experienced group leaders—and challenges us to apply our best skills in many areas, from administration to safety, teambuilding to pastoral care, and ethics to theology. Use this book to educate yourself and the congregation—and have fun! Welcome to the journey

Two

Some Big Questions

> It is in our liberal religious bloodline to gather and organize ourselves as a prophetic church, a religious community that seeks to intervene in human history for the sake of social justice.
>
> —Richard S. Gilbert

A mission trip is a big undertaking—and it is essential that planning begin with a committed group of people. Perhaps a member of your congregation has suggested the idea of mission work to the Board, or the idea grew out of the Social Action Committee. Perhaps the youth group has decided they want to "go somewhere and do something." Whatever the structure and size of your congregation, you will need direct support of the trip from a congregational committee (e.g., Religious Education Committee, Social Action Committee, Governing Board) to connect the experience with the mission and vision of the congregation. Whether your aim is to develop the support of a sponsoring committee or to explore the commitment of a group of potential participants, posing a series of questions for reflection and sharing will help you shape your experience and identify meaningful goals. This chapter presents some core questions.

Why Should a Congregation Do a Mission Trip with Youth?

Philosophically speaking, a mission trip has several objectives. One is to involve members of a congregation in direct social action work. Another is to provide a catalyst for increasing the congregation's engagement in direct social action over the long term—action that is hands-on, multigenerational, and often interfaith. The group will learn experientially what it means to become a caring community and how service work reflects its faith.

While the logistics of a mission trip can be daunting, the preparation helps the group explore the many relational dynamics of what it means to be a caring community. Including the entire congregation—members of all ages—in significant inquiry will spark insights into how to treat others with dignity. Engaging the congregation in planning for the trip can lay the groundwork for participants to discover how to live in solidarity with people in need outside the congregation—who are the center of the mission trip.

People's reasons for doing a mission trip are many and varied. This is normal, especially within a group of youth. Some youth just want to "get away" or seek an impressive experience for their college applications. Some want to help people, while others want to escape the stresses of their own lives. Still others do not know why they want to go and are following the crowd.

A strong group leader can convert this range of reasons into energy for a journey with purpose. Once you articulate the premise and parameters of the trip and establish the ground rules of respect for a group covenant, you will be well on your way toward establishing a shared vision for the mission. Then it is likely all participants will have a valuable experience that exceeds their expectations.

A mission trip builds Unitarian Universalist faith identity

Programmatically speaking, youth need opportunities that will help them define and articulate their beliefs as Unitarian Universalists. Experiential learning trips provide them with a chance to demonstrate and test those beliefs in a real-life setting. Then they will integrate their mission trip experiences into their personal faith identity. Additionally, leadership opportunities abound for youth on a mission trip. Stepping out of their everyday world, they develop new skills that support their faith development as young Unitarian Universalists dedicated to a cause.

Likewise, offering the congregation a chance to observe youth as they prepare for the journey engages curiosity and promotes widespread investment in the youth's experience. When the mission and goals of the trip are presented to the congregation as a relevant topic of faith exploration, ideas for additional ways for the entire congregation to explore the mission's goals arise.

Spiritually speaking, a mission trip offers youth the chance to bring together the desire to do good deeds with a compelling action based on spiritual values. These values offer a lasting connection to Unitarian Universalist Principles and nurture a person's developing faith identity. Having the group understand and agree to the faith-based parameters of the trip is important to ensure a unified experience rather than just rendering fragmented services. What might begin as an act of charity can develop into a lifelong commitment to justice.

What Type of Mission Work Do You Want to Do?

Find out about organizations that facilitate or provide mission trip experiences. Learn about the work they do and how mission teams can be involved. It is essential to identify an organization and an experience that will be a good fit for your group. Weigh each organization's mission trip options against what you know about your group and its goals. Are you looking to develop relationships with the people you will be helping, or with an organization that provides service? Do you want to achieve an end product such as by building a house, or do you hope to provide relief services such as getting food and clean water to people in disaster areas? Are special skills required for the work you want to do? For instance, if you are planning to do relief work, what qualifications, skills, or special preparations will members need to go into a setting where people have experienced trauma or disaster?

How Do You Choose an Organization?

Seek organizations that best match the skill set and expressed vision of your team. If you know your group wants to use building skills, consider an organization whose projects develop and utilize those skills. If your group wants to engage directly with a marginalized group, find an organization that serves that population. For specific suggestions, see Organizations That Work with Mission Teams on page 75.

Contact religious professionals at other congregations who might have experience with the organizations that interest you. Although each trip is different, the recommendations of other groups or leaders can help you narrow your search. Researching the organizations online will help clarify your range of choices. Look on organizations' websites for testimonials from leaders and participants and for practical tools such as checklists and information sheets, similar to those found in the Resources section of this book.

Logistical considerations must come first. Find out which organizations offer a mission trip experience that will suit your group in terms of cost, time frame, age of the participants, and group size.

Cost

Organizations that provide mission trips charge a wide range of fees. Determine the exact cost of a trip and the services included in the price. Also, research additional expenses participants will incur, such as the costs of transportation, food, and lodging, that the organization does not provide. Include the total likely cost, or an informed estimate, in the initial information packet for participants. You must give youth and their parents the information they need to determine whether the mission trip is affordable. Also consider whether the group will do any fundraising and to what extent the funds raised can underwrite the cost of the trip, perhaps to assist participants who otherwise could not afford to go.

Time frame

To schedule a mission trip, you must know when youth are available to participate. Use these questions to determine the best time for a trip:

- Can the youth go only during school vacation? Do all the potential participants have common school vacation periods?
- Could you make the trip while school is in session? If so, when would be best?
- Will schools expect and/or allow students to make up days of school and work they miss? Will youth need a letter requesting an extension for school assignments?

Then, identify organizations that fit your parameters. Find out:

- Does the organization you hope to work with accommodate groups throughout the year or only at specific times of year?
- How much additional time will the group need for travel to and from the destination?

Age and group size limitations

Some organizations have minimum age requirements, require a certain youth-to-adult ratio, or have a maximum and/or minimum group size. Learn about these requirements or restrictions. Other factors that can vary considerably, and that might affect the size and configuration of the group you will bring, include

- type of ground transportation (e.g., the seating capacity of vans)
- type of accommodations
- availability of group airfares
- size-defined projects (for example, many home-building missions require a specific number of participants to complete a project).

What Do You Hope to Gain from This Experience?

A mission trip serves as its own religious education curriculum with a real-life impact. Experiential learning gives participants a chance to meet individuals who may have significantly less power, privilege, and material wealth than they do. With this ultimate vision in mind, articulating the objectives and goals for the group early on will help cultivate

- close relationships and a deeper group connection
- an understanding of how this work connects to and deepens an individual's Unitarian Universalist lifespan faith development and identity
- a foundation for continued justice work
- incentive for utilizing skills learned while serving locally
- opportunities to increase participation in future mission trips
- leadership skills to enrich the congregation
- experience and learning to integrate into the congregation.

The core questions presented in this chapter require significant reflection. They will help you discern the objectives of your team and then match them with the mission of a particular organization, so you can provide an experience consistent with your group's abilities, vision, and goals.

THREE

Mission Trip Building Blocks

> By working in this manner,
> For the sake of the land and people
> To be in vital relation with each other,
> We will have life,
> And it will continue.
>
> —SIMON ORTIZ

"We need to get out there and do some good in the world," say many mission trip participants who are motivated to get started. The following process, while not in any fixed order, represents key elements to address to convert that sentiment into reality.

After you research organizations and choose one that will meet the needs of your group, it is time to publicize the mission and its purpose at every opportunity, including religious education, worship, and other congregational gatherings.

Build and Nurture Congregational Support

Congregational support for a mission trip is vital, whether the work is an expression of the congregation's mission or a component of religious education programming. The level of support you achieve will influence your ability to dedicate staff time and resources to the mission trip, and may influence the extent to which the congregation both actively participates in fundraising and devotes time in worship for relevant faith explorations.

Identify a Group Leader

Mission trips offer the potential for transformative experiences that give context and possibility to lifespan religious education. The skills required to lead mission trips call for the group leader to be a religious professional (minister, religious educator, or staff youth advisor), a qualified adult lay member of the congregation, or a youth leader under the advisement of a religious professional, staff member, or other qualified adult. The standards, training, and resources provided by the Unitarian Universalist Association to religious professionals supply the framework for this sacred work. Responsibility and liability are best carried by staff members who manage details like these as part of their jobs and who will ultimately be accountable to participants, their families, and the sponsoring institution. No doubt, many aspects of trip planning can and should be delegated to group members. Yet coordinating a trip requires a significant amount of oversight.

Identify the Mission Team

It is difficult to proceed with the possibility of a Unitarian Universalist youth-based mission trip without making some assumptions about who will go. The very notion of a "trip" may create a feeling of exclusion in youth and families who would like to be part of serving yet cannot afford a trip they might consider a luxury. Our anti-oppression work requires an acute commitment to ongoing examination of our values, in every aspect of our lives. As part of our faith work, we Unitarian Universalists are called to hold each other responsible for making sure the meaning of *we* reflects the true population of the group. Specifically, how a week away will affect family systems of childcare, employment (especially self-employment), financial resources, and other care issues requires serious group consideration. The planning stages of a trip offer the congregation an early opportunity to become committed stewards of its members. The moment we leave someone behind because of an unfair standard, we fail.

There are many ways to configure a team, and each has its benefits. For example, a predominantly youth-based trip offers an ultimate experience for a faith-based youth group. At the same time, the possibility or requirement for a parent to accompany their child on a trip can create a unifying experience in the fabric of the family's life. A mission team can mirror a congregation's multigenerational approach and commitment to social action if the trip is offered to both youth and adults.

Youth-based trips will ideally have a 1:4 adult-to-youth ratio; many organizations that provide mission trips use this standard. Adult leaders will both participate in the mission work and guide youth through an experience that will be both challenging and spiritually rewarding. The leaders' skills and experience must support these responsibilities. Establish criteria for how you will recruit adults before you extend the call for youth participants. Be sure that an adult's group skills and temperament match with the group.

Partner with Parents and Caregivers

Leading a group of youth on a mission trip is a huge responsibility and a big honor. Trip leaders will be accompanying youth on a faith journey, empowering youth to expand their worldview, and serving as a critical link to their families. For parents and caregivers to grant permission for youth to participate in a trip, they must have confidence in the adult leadership or, when youth leaders are planning a trip, the adults who are advising them. Parent and caregiver confidence is necessary before, during, and after the trip.

Include parents and caregivers in the communication loop. They need reliable information about all aspects of the trip that require their support and involvement, from permission forms and payment procedures to the plans and schedules they need to support their youth's full participation in all planning meetings, fundraisers, related events, and the trip itself.

A mission trip provides a unique opportunity for youth to develop leadership skills. While clear and effective communication is a skill we hope youth will develop, remember that youth skill-building is a work in progress. Adult group leaders and advisors should not delegate to youth the sole responsibility of communicating trip details to their parents and caregivers.

FOUR

The Journey Begins

Blessed are the poor in spirit: for theirs is the kingdom of heaven.
Blessed are they that mourn: for they shall be comforted.
Blessed are the meek: for they shall inherit the earth.
Blessed are they who hunger and thirst after righteousness: for they shall be filled.
Blessed are the merciful: for they shall obtain mercy.
Blessed are the pure in heart: for they shall see God.
Blessed are the peacemakers: for they shall be called the children of God.

—MATTHEW 5:3–9

Now it is time to begin the faith work of team building and covenanting, establishing a system of raising sacred dollars, and educating the team about the mission and the justice issues it touches.

Team Building

The benefits you reap from a mission trip, like other life experiences, are directly related to what you are willing to invest. The opportunities to learn and explore are endless, as are the opportunities for leadership development, making a mission trip a perfect exercise in religious education. Choosing the issues you want to investigate and dividing responsibilities among participants will shape participants' experience before you even leave your congregation. Our intentions while doing this work provide us, as Unitarian Universalists, the opportunity to explore what it means to do the work as an expression of our faith.

This will be a journey for each individual, as well as for the group as a whole. While recognizing that groups can come together in a variety of ways to engage in mission work, it is necessary to cultivate a strong team identity in order to move forward as a cohesive group. The passage from making an individual commitment to engaging in a larger group commitment is one of the first transformations a participant will undergo on this journey.

Groups progress through a variety of stages as individuals get to know each other and a sense of community begins to develop. As a leader, you can facilitate the group to begin building relationships on a strong foundation of trust, identity, and shared sense of purpose. The incremental steps of building a group dynamic are essential for creating a successful and fun experience. The Resources section of this book offers some tools that may be helpful; see Covenanting, Team-Building Games, and Five Steps of Community Building.

Covenant

One step in planning a mission trip journey is to discern and name the different covenants—explicit and implied—that are part of the mission. The first place to covenant explicitly is in the creation of shared expectations. As the group deepens its relationships and gets ready for the physical journey, a second opportunity to covenant will present itself in response to the unique circumstances of the trip. When this happens, the group can revisit the first covenant and adapt it as needed.

For a youth-based trip, the adult leader—or a youth leader with the help of an advisor—must explicitly state in writing, as a contract, expectations regarding

- behavior guidelines during trip preparation and the trip itself
- the nature of work requirements for trip preparations and mission tasks

- attendance at meetings
- participation in trip activities, including reflection time.

Cliques

The existence of cliques, particularly in youth groups, can present an implicit covenant that can make or break the success of the trip. The tendency of youth to gravitate toward team members who are their friends can create a hurtful, possibly traumatic experience for a youth who needs help creating relationships and becoming part of a group. Do not proceed with the notion that issues of preference and exclusion will "work themselves out"; this will leave everyone frustrated and limit the success of the mission. At a mission's core is the call to walk toward areas of personal discomfort and intolerance. This is how participants encounter new experiences, outside the boundaries of the beliefs and structures of our day-to-day lives.

Whether cliques are addressed explicitly in the creation of a covenant or have already been addressed within the youth group, guidance and firm expectations will ensure the comfort and social safety that adolescents need. Some ways to address cliques are:

- Facilitate small group discussions to explore issues of teen identity and acceptance.
- Suggest games and exercises that encourage spontaneous relationship development.
- Implement creative ways to change groupings, such as counting, alphabetizing, pre-establishing clusters, interests, and the like.

Determining the Financial Needs of Team Members

Perhaps one of the most important elements of organizing a mission trip is coming to terms with how it will be paid for. Individuals can respond to money matters in complex ways, requiring sensitivity and thoughtful navigation. Be forewarned that how you define the financial needs of the group and of individuals will influence all aspects of planning and the overall experience.

While the focus of a mission may be directed at issues of justice, give the same attention to the reality of economic justice within the group. Starting with the first dollar you and your team members raise and pay, remember the second Principle that Unitarian Universalist congregations affirm: justice, equity, and compassion in human relations. The amount of money each individual contributes to their trip expenses should not affect the group covenant.

It is incumbent on a skilled group leader or youth advisor to level the playing field for anyone interested in participating. Creating a process that allows team members to state their financial need in a confidential way is part of the group leader's work. At the same time, all team members should be fully informed about the impact that subsidizing trip costs will have on the group. The rest is mostly process and faith.

Individual financial circumstances and varying attitudes of scarcity and generosity will come into play. You will want to find a respectful way to help participants, their families, and your congregation to weigh personal or community financial need against the larger issues of economic justice faced by the organization you are supporting. While it is true that many people have little or no disposable income in the current economy, many do have financial resources far greater than the individuals and groups who will be served on the trip. Bring that perspective to participants and families, and encourage them to define their needs by the amount without which they would be unable to participate in the trip. Invite them to differentiate between what they would like to pay and what they are able to pay.

Will group members be expected to pay their own costs or will financial assistance be available? If the latter, how will you handle participants' different financial needs? Some participants will be able to pay their entire trip expense, while others may need a full scholarship, and still others will fall somewhere in between. You will want to address sensitive financial issues while respecting privacy. The table below lists four possible approaches to addressing issues of financial assistance.

Self-Selecting
Each participant is expected to pay the full amount.

Congregational Subsidy
A congregation fund provides assistance to those who are unable to pay the full amount.

Group-Assisted
On a slip of paper, participants write the amount of assistance they need; the total represents the team fundraising goal.

Solidarity
On a slip of paper, participants write the amount of assistance they need; multiply the highest amount by the number of participants; the product represents the team fundraising goal. Any difference between what is needed and what is raised provides the basis for a donation to the organization you will be working with.

Raising Sacred Dollars

If participants need significant financial assistance, you may question whether it is worth doing the mission trip at all. Some people might advocate for raising money and sending it directly to the organization instead. However, remember that a willingness to bear witness to the oppression and injustice experienced by marginalized groups is fundamental to mission work, which in turn provides an authentic catalyst for its participants to work toward systemic change. Organizations that work with mission groups do so in a shared commitment to lifting humanity through real interactions, even when it might be faster and cheaper to hire contractors to do the work.

Whether participants' families, the congregational budget, or a large-scale fundraising effort pay for it, a mission trip represents an investment in much more than the tasks it will accomplish and the community those tasks will help. The funds that enable a mission trip also enable a potentially life-changing experience for each participant—an experience that can nurture faith development and energize a lifelong commitment to service and justice.

Regardless of how you will raise funds, as a group you need to clearly articulate how you will use the funds you raise. Will you use them to support individual participants? The overall cost of the trip? The organization you are supporting? Establish the amount of money you need to raise. Then consider what to do with any funds you may raise beyond your goal. Some organizations' program fees already include a financial contribution to their mission; even so, your group could choose to make a donation exceeding an organization's suggestion or requirement.

After you determine the fundraising goal, decide whether you will require team members to participate in all fundraising events, regardless of their ability to pay for their portion of the trip. Full group participation will add to the team-building aspect of the experience and engage youth in the work of economic justice in their own community.

When planning fundraising, think about events that have been financially successful in your congregation that you can adapt to educate people about the mission. For instance, suppose your mission trip will support an organization that works to end poverty in a particular community, and groups in your congregation have sponsored terrific potluck or spaghetti suppers in the past. You might organize a supper, using as a model the Hunger Banquet created by Oxfam International (www.oxfam.org). Such an event would satisfy the dual goals of raising funds for the trip and increasing your congregation's awareness of your mission.

There are numerous ways to fundraise, from bake sales, car washes, and pancake breakfasts to coffee houses, raffles, and auctions. Be creative! You might even consider options that expand the support for your trip beyond the walls of your congregation.

Understanding the Mission and the Justice Issues Involved

While each mission team member has their own reasons for participating, a shared understanding of the particular mission work you will do helps ground the experience with the vision. Practical questions like those that follow take on significance as the group prepares for its journey.

What do we know about the organization we are supporting?
You and your team must learn as much as possible about the organization you'll be working with, including the nature of the issues they address. Will you be visiting a developing country, or an inner-city neighborhood? Think about what you might need to know as a guest in someone else's country or community. Who in the organization will introduce you to the community where you will be working? What experience and relationships does that person have?

Explore any external factors, perhaps unrelated to your planned mission work, that affect the circumstances of the population served by the organization. For example, if your group plans to help build a school in a rural village, find out whether the village has clean, running water and what crops or industries form the basis of its economy. Be informed and ready to talk with the group about what these factors mean for you as Unitarian Universalists, as Americans, and, perhaps, as people of privilege.

How are health and safety issues addressed?
If you are traveling to a different country, you and your group may be required or encouraged to receive special immunizations. You will find information about health risks specific to world regions at the World Health Organization (WHO) website, www.who.int. The Centers for Disease Control also maintains current immunization recommendations online, www.cdc.gov.

Although common sense and knowing cultural customs will help ensure a safe trip abroad, remember that risk is inherent in all travel. The U.S. Department of State website, www.state.gov, posts specific safety concerns and travel advisories. Encourage group members and their families to visit this and the WHO website before departing on the trip. Group members will likely find detailed descriptions of crime reports for your country of destination; note that such information may or may not helpfully indicate the relative safety of your destination.

How will we get there?

Your modes of transportation, both to your destination and while you are there, will be a function of group size and expense. Whether you travel by van, bus, train, plane, rental vehicle, or some other means, learn what kinds of travel insurance are available (or required) and research whether it is worthwhile. If traveling by air, work with a travel agent to investigate a group discount. Make these arrangements as far in advance as possible.

What will we need while we are there?

Organizations that work with mission groups will have a list of suggested and required items to pack, such as clothing, special gear, food, tools, and so on. Be sure to follow the packing list carefully. Once you are at your destination, you might regret choosing not to bring an item when you discover that it is both necessary and unavailable where you are. (For more on this topic, see Chapter 5, "What to Pack," on page 26.)

Building Awareness and Tolerance of Cultural Differences

Learning how to be a guest in another culture is a valuable educational opportunity, and that dynamic can play out at every juncture. You might be working with other youth as part of your mission project. Those youth may be part of a Unitarian Universalist youth group like yours, from another denomination, or local to the area where the mission is. In all cases, be mindful of cultural differences that will influence your interactions. When a project includes youth from different youth groups, a leader must be ready to practice skilled facilitation to guide a process of understanding each other's differences and articulating the common cause.

How do faith and religion play into this experience?
As you prepare for the trip it will be useful to know whether the organization you are supporting is faith-based or secular. If it is faith-based, learn how its religious affiliation will affect your experience. Determine the extent to which you will find opportunity for interfaith collaboration around a common cause. If this is not possible, find out what your group needs to learn about the host's religion and/or culture to prepare to be guests. If the organization is secular, establish that your host will honor your intention to have group reflection time grounded in Unitarian Universalist spirituality.

In an interfaith group, create opportunities for participants and others involved in the mission work to express their faith, rather than avoiding references to differing theologies. In some cases, conduct research and lead a group discussion ahead of time so the group can air their questions and learn a bit about what to expect. It is not uncommon for a local family or faith community to invite a mission team into a local custom. Prepare the team to respond with the utmost care, respect, and appreciation. Such an occasion can invite youth into a memorable experience of holy contemplation and worship.

FIVE

Packing Your Bags

With resources scarcer and scarcer
  I vow with all beings
To consider the law of proportion:
  My have is another's have-not.
—ROBERT AITKEN

You will want to be prepared with every resource you may need on the mission trip—physically, emotionally, and spiritually. This chapter will help you pack with care.

Prepare for the Unexpected

As a leader traveling with a group in unfamiliar territory, it is always a good idea to prepare for the unexpected. What if a participant gets sick, someone loses a wallet, or luggage does not arrive when and where it is supposed to? While these are the types of experiences we all could do without, the unexpected can occur in minor or major ways and hugely affect the trip. Good planning helps minimize the impact of unexpected problems. For instance, will you carry a first aid kit? Where will you keep copies of emergency contact information? How will you safeguard important travel documents? If your accommodations will be off-site or participants plan to travel beyond the scope of the mission, how will you contact the organization you are working with should the youth be unable to return to the site when expected? With thoughtful planning, unexpected obstacles can be handled with minimum stress and will leave participants with nothing more than an interesting story to tell.

What to Pack

Some organizations provide a specific packing list and an instruction to pack only what is on the list. Be sure to review the list with your group, and take the organization's recommendations seriously. Other organizations may suggest only the items you might not think of, such as tools specifically needed for the mission or personal care items you may be unable to purchase in the destination area.

If the organization does not provide a detailed packing list, consider making a checklist for your group. A detailed list will help all participants pack essential items and minimize over-packing.

Consider:

- What will the climate and local terrain be like?
- Will you need warm- or cold-weather clothing?
- Will you need rain gear?
- What type of footwear is appropriate?
- What are the local customs of dress? When are/aren't shorts and T-shirts appropriate?
- What clothes are suitable for the mission trip work?
- What is considered appropriate attire for attending worship?
- Are different customs in place for male and female attire?
- Will you need special tools and/or supplies?
- Will you need gifts for your hosts?
- What might you need for a side trip off-site?

Advise youth to pack only what is on the list and to avoid bringing additional items. Mention the obvious items to exclude, such as recreational drugs and alcohol, as well as inappropriate clothing and personal electronics. Depending on the organization's rules and local laws, arriving with certain items can earn participants a quick return home or, even worse, a visit to a local jail.

What to Leave at Home

Some youth and adults are accustomed to traveling with personal electronic devices such as cell phones, iPods, and laptops. However, not everyone can afford these luxury items. Before your group departs on a journey, set a parameter that will support an equitable group identity; this is an important part of your mission.

Additionally, bringing expensive, luxury items to an impoverished region increases the potential for theft. These items might unintentionally project a pretentious and perhaps inaccurate image of mission trip participants belonging to an affluent and privileged culture. Although electronics and other accoutrements are commonplace in middle-class culture, bringing them on a mission trip can limit the opportunity to meet others in openness, dignity, and equality.

Therefore, regardless of the destination or length of your mission trip, we strongly recommend a "no electronics" rule. Enforcing this rule sets the tone for a journey in which participants must prepare for the unknown together. Because they will not be distracted by their electronics, youth can engage more fully with each other, those with whom they are working, and their surroundings.

The rule should have two exceptions: (1) Group leaders should have access to a cell phone for parents and caregivers to call *only* in the event of an emergency. (2) Participants should be allowed to pack cameras. Making a visual record of the mission trip will sharpen the experience for some participants, capture memories that some will treasure for years to come, and facilitate sharing the experience when your group returns home.

Prior to your departure, be sure to have a dedicated discussion about camera use. Discuss how and when taking pictures might be considered inappropriate or disrespectful. Some cultures and communities (especially those that are struggling) may not share your enthusiasm for documenting your experience. Some may even show hostility. Although documenting the experience can be a powerful way to bring the journey home to share with others, some profound moments should not be intruded on with a camera nor shared with outsiders.

Appoint a Medic

Your packing list should include specific instructions for how prescription and over-the-counter medications will be managed. Assuming that youth participants are minors, it is advisable to designate one adult to serve as the "trip medic" who will hold and manage all medications. This will facilitate recordkeeping, transporting and/or administering medications, and keeping tabs on the well-being of all participants. Appointing a medic also reduces the possibility of loss or misuse of medications and minimizes lapses in taking medications that can occur when people are outside their everyday routines. A medic can also facilitate efficient response and clear communication in the event of an emergency. Before departing on your mission trip, decide whether the medic or group leader will be responsible for forms such as emergency contacts, medical insurance information, passports, and other travel documents.

Practice Makes Perfect

Reduce the chances of participants forgetting to bring important items by holding a group packing session two or three weeks before your departure date. At this meeting, go over last-minute questions about things to bring or things to leave at home. To make the session fun, have the group prepare for a particular day on their itinerary. For example, should they pack for a travel day or a work day? What is the appropriate attire? Do they need to pack special tools or supplies? If so, do they know where the objects are located? A practice session will not guarantee that everyone will arrive at the destination with all the right supplies—but it will help. And it will demonstrate how an individual's organization, preparation, and attention to detail can affect the overall team experience.

Know the Conditions You Will Face

If you will be working in an impoverished community or an area that was devastated by a natural disaster, learn about the conditions of the area and how they affect the population. If you are able, talk with organization representatives or other volunteers who have traveled to your destination. No amount of reading or hearing secondhand accounts can completely prepare you for experiencing those conditions firsthand, but your effort will provide a context for participants and lessen the chance of their feeling overwhelmed. Group members may still have responses that need pastoral support. Know in advance which team leaders have the skills to pastorally support participants.

Being a Guest in Another Community

Whatever the individual motivations that brought them into the group, everyone on the team must prepare to be a guest in another culture. Engage your team in explicit conversations ahead of time. Encourage them to "think different" before making any assumptions while on the trip. Assumptions, however small, about a community and its circumstances can lead to stereotyping and baseless judgments and take away from the deep learning that often occurs while on mission. Recognizing this possibility up front offers an opportunity to define the experience in a more positive way. Participants' awareness that they are guests in another culture will fuel their transformation; this is a primary impetus for undertaking a social justice mission.

Your team can learn a great deal from people in other communities and cultures. Prepare the participants to consciously open themselves to this opportunity. Before you travel, lead in-depth discussions about assumptions, cultural norms and messages, customs, manners, and cultural appropriation. Guide the team to treat unfamiliar sights and scenes with utmost respect and to conduct themselves appropriately in situations that are new for them.

Find out about local customs of dress and take them seriously. Make no assumptions. For example, in a culture where jeans and T-shirts are acceptable, local residents may take offense at T-shirts with provocative or political words or images. Acceptable attire within one community or age group may be highly offensive and unacceptable in another.

Caution the group to avoid making assumptions about behavioral norms, especially regarding expressions of affection. In some cultures and communities, it is inappropriate for a male and female to touch or hug. Other areas for discussion may include table manners, language, and gestures. Consult your sponsoring organization for specific guidance and encourage team members to do their own research to share with the group.

Continuous Community Building

Nurturing a sense of community among your group should begin in the earliest planning stages. Yet it is also vital to take time during the trip to keep the group focused on a shared vision and well-being. In the midst of busy travel and work days, make time to come together for guided group reflection. Make sure you provide the emotional and spiritual space to take care of individuals and the group.

Community building happens differently during the trip than before it. At home, during the planning and preparation stages, our daily routines and preoccupations with family, work, and school limit our ability to come together. The experience of a mission trip is powerfully different. Develop and implement expectations, systems, and rituals to bring the group together each day of the trip. This is a key element of taking care of each person on the team.

Spiritual Reflection on Your Trip

Given that this trip is part of a faith-based journey, bring a spiritual aspect into the work you do on the trip. Scheduled downtime is not, by itself, enough. Dedicated time for reflection or check-in

—facilitated on a regular basis by a group leader—provides participants with a needed opportunity to express how they are doing. The Resources section on page 73 provides a variety of tools to help you shape intentional, spiritual time for the group before, during, and after the trip.

Consider lighting a chalice at the beginning of your meetings. Take time to check in with one another. Make opportunities for team members to talk about what they are fearful of and what they are most excited about. Encouraging deeper sharing is a way to further develop the bonds between participants.

Daily check-in meetings will allow group leaders to gauge the emotional well-being of participants. You could also share a short worship service. At the very least, encourage participants to journal daily by providing journal prompts or scheduling a dedicated quiet time for the group to write. In addition to being a great way for participants to process what they are experiencing, journals provide an invaluable resource for participants to reflect on their experience after the trip. The Journaling resource on page 115 provides a rationale for making journaling a regular part of the team's spiritual practice on a mission trip and offers journal prompts for before, during, and after the trip.

Of course, take time during the trip to celebrate your commitment to making the world a better place!

Packing Your Bags with Fun

With a firmly arranged plan and mission in place, do not forget time for having fun. Have no doubt that youth will color their experience with fun. As a group leader, be ready to recognize, if not create, space for fun moments "off the page." If an experience is getting too intense, initiate a break. Pull out a game, a song, or simply a ball. You can allow unscheduled joy and fun to fill the space without disrupting other important elements of maintaining a cohesive group. It is a true balancing act, but a discerning and watchful eye can look for potential magical moments.

Six

Who's in Charge?

> We have only begun to know
> the power that is in us if we would join
> our solitudes in the communion of struggle.
>
> —Denise Levertov

Processing the complex question about who is in charge can take many hours. However, it is an important topic for creating a transformative experience, particularly for youth. The planning and other tasks involved in undertaking a mission trip are not to be underestimated. Even the most skilled group leader cannot do everything, and carefully considering the delegation of tasks is one of the major planning pieces of the entire project.

Consider, for example, the checklist required for a team to simply get on a plane heading from Boston, Massachusetts, to Guatemala—before the actual mission work even begins.

- Select an organization.
- Prepare and lead an information session.
- Choose adult advisors.
- Distribute and collect required forms.
- Obtain necessary travel documents.
- Organize trip finances and accounting.
- Plan and lead fundraisers.
- Arrange airfare and ground transportation.
- Arrange accommodations.
- Obtain or create a packing list.

- Assemble an emergency phone number list for parents.
- Address health and safety issues.
- Compile a list of participant food allergies and restrictions.
- List and obtain necessary equipment and supplies.
- Plan how to keep the congregation informed and involved (e.g., set up a phone tree or email lists, designate a leader to update Facebook daily).

A paid staff person does not have enough time to handle all the administrative tasks, consider educational aspects, and lead the team-building process. The adult and youth leadership team should divide the workload, to properly prepare the group and to maintain everyone's sanity. This is an opportunity to cultivate lay leadership on many levels.

The role of the trip leader(s), first and foremost, is to protect the physical and emotional safety of each group member. While both adults and youth will be able to make significant contributions, it is critical for the group leader to discern which skills, tasks, and responsibilities are appropriate for both youth and adults. In the end, the adults and the group leader are responsible—and liable—for the safety and well-being of minors. Not every adult will have the skills necessary to hold such responsibility, but they will still be able to contribute in a valuable way.

The environment surrounding a mission trip is different from our home environments. The completion of basic daily tasks by a large group takes more time than we might anticipate. Develop effective organizational systems before embarking on the trip to minimize the time you will spend figuring out logistics during the mission.

Perhaps the group already has a shared understanding or a formal covenant about individual liberties when the group is together. Even so, the agreement about individual liberties will be different in the context of a mission trip. The way youth operate in their congregational youth groups and their homes is likely more fluid and relaxed than what will be necessary on a trip. Take the time to discuss the range of expectations for the trip and create a new set of liberties. For example, the moment travel begins, the adults on a trip are responsible for the minors, and must be able to account for the whereabouts of every team member, at every moment. This understanding should be explicit among trip leaders, youth, and parents and caretakers.

Legally, adults are mandated to be in charge because they are liable for minors' safety on a trip. At the same time, our Unitarian Universalist Principles and practices support adults mentoring youth into appropriate leadership roles, and many youth have extensive experience and can take the initiative to lead peers within the model of youth empowerment. However, the intensity of mission work is unlike that of a congregational or district-sponsored youth conference. Because mission work has the goal of personal and spiritual transformation in new environments, it takes us beyond our comfort zone. Even if a youth seems abundantly capable, it is not wise to put them in a position of overwhelming responsibility. Youth should not expect to take responsibility for more than their share of caring for and leading others while doing mission work. There will be opportunities to foster developmentally appropriate leadership skills among youth—before, during, and after the mission trip—without compromising the safety of the youth or the group.

The teenage capacity to integrate a new experience and function in a new setting will vary from person to person, as it does with adults. Adult leaders ideally should have a basic understanding of adolescent development so they can best support youth's growth in leadership. Here are some tips for adult leaders:

- Look for ways to teach leadership explicitly by sharing tasks.
- Look for opportunities to respond to leadership initiatives by the youth.
- Encourage collaboration.
- Be clear that the adults are responsible.
- Never compromise on safety.
- Maximize layers of accountability.

A mission team must function as a unit in which all members share accountability for the group. One practical way to ensure the overall team's accountability is to organize youth into smaller identity groups. Identity group leaders can facilitate conversations, convey information from the trip leader, and count heads to help keep track of youth.

Staying in Touch

Before you leave on your mission trip, have a plan in place for notifying parents of your arrival at your destination. One way is to set up an email distribution list. When you arrive, call or email the church administrator, who will email parents and caregivers with the news of your safe arrival. For mission trips longer than a week, provide parents and your congregation's office with a contact number (e.g., your cell phone or the hosting organization's office number) where they can reach you in the event of an emergency. Given an option, some parents and caregivers and some youth may want to be in touch more often, so be explicit if contact information is for emergencies only. While staying in touch with family and friends may seem innocuous, frequent calls can jar the rhythm of both the group and the trip and keep youth from fully integrating into the experience.

If youth want to be in touch more frequently, encourage them to write postcards or letters. These will help youth process their experiences at a deeper level, without inviting the distraction of an immediate response. You may need to make other arrangements for trips that are longer in duration. Investigate whether Internet cafés are available at your destination. A group leader might also drop a letter in the mail as the mission trip begins, describing elements of the trip and preparing parents for post-trip dynamics and challenges.

Coping with Homesickness and Other Discomforts

Emotional outbursts, stomach aches or headaches, and withdrawn behavior all can be symptoms of homesickness. As your trip unfolds, watch for participants who may be homesick. Be aware which youth are away from home without family for the first time.

For others—youth and adults, new and seasoned travelers alike—the trip itself can bring physical, emotional, or spiritual discomfort. Coming face to face with extreme poverty or other types of oppression can disturb some people to the point of a physical response.

It is natural for participants to experience some degree of emotional upheaval during a mission trip. While disturbing feelings often fuel a participant's transformation as a result of the trip, it would be a mistake to leave such feelings unattended during the trip. The group must include at least one adult leader skilled at providing pastoral support. In most instances, a pastoral conversation in which a youth or adult feels heard, and held, will bolster them to gather their internal resources and continue on with the mission experience. However, the leader should be ready to discern when a youth needs to call their parents or caregivers back home, or possibly even leave the trip.

Acting Out

A youth mission team will comprise a range of personalities and behaviors. You can expect to see some acting out as team members adjust to an intense group experience and respond to the culture shock of poverty or disaster. However, the team also needs limits. One person's demands for attention or acute need for one-on-one support has the potential to ruin the group's overall experience.

Taking time for team-building and thoughtful covenanting before the trip is the best way to prevent unfortunate incidents, but does not rule out the possibility of challenging behavior. Have a clear plan in place to address behavior that disrupts the group experience and mission focus. Be prepared to give immediate feedback, including clear choices and consequences, to any participant who acts out. If necessary, isolate the individual to protect the rest of the group.

A group's covenant or contract that states behavior expectations can also identify the processes and consequences the team will use to address inappropriate behavior on the trip. For example, a covenant might specify the situations in which the team will meet and decide by consensus whether a participant's behavior warrants a phone call to parents or caretakers at home.

Four Stages: Separation, Transition, Transformation and Re-entry

A mission trip is a physical, emotional, and spiritual journey. It is a pilgrimage of sorts, on which we travel some distance and submit ourselves to conditions and experiences that are likely very different from anything we've ever experienced. Some define the term *pilgrimage* as a journey of risk and promise. One risk is that we may undergo personal change. Such change can also be viewed as a promise.

Every participant, including leaders, will pass through several stages during this journey. First, you separate—from home, routine, and the familiar surroundings and support systems of your life. There is discomfort in this separation as you leave behind the comfortable and prepare for the unknown.

In the next stage of the journey, you transition into the mission experience. You open to it. You get down to the work you have signed on to do. At this stage, you may find yourself reaching for the internal resources to do physical, emotional, or spiritual tasks you are not sure you can do or for which you have doubts about your preparedness. Some people will tap their internal resources on their own, perhaps instinctively; others may need support from leaders or peers in the group. During the transition stage, you also absorb culture shock. The rhythm and routine of the day may unfold in a way that feels unfamiliar or uncomfortable. The shock may occur as the abstract concept of the mission emerges, before your eyes, into a tangible reality. Transitioning from having intellectual discussions about poverty to being surrounded by it in a sensory, visceral way can be a shock. Your experience of culture shock can touch the heart of what it means for you to be of service to and to be in relationship with others.

As the mission proceeds, you will move into the third stage of the journey, personal transformation. While each participant's transformation experience will happen in its own way, toward its own end, on its own timetable, some transformation is almost inevitable. After all, youth are traveling—perhaps for the first time—as part of a group, to a new place with new people where they will undertake a service mission that will never be repeated in exactly the same way. They will come face to face with people in a way that forces them to accept both their common humanity and their stark differences in circumstances. The experience of bearing witness to oppression can, in itself, spark transformation. Each team member's transformation will be fed and shaped as they develop new relationships within and outside your mission team, practice seeing the world in a different way, learn and practice new skills, and gain insights into themselves and their connections with the world.

The final stage of the journey is re-entry—returning home to a familiar place, routine, and relationships. Although slipping back into the familiar might seem an easy thing to do, re-entry can be difficult. Youth may have complex, even hostile reactions to friends' and families' typical questions such as "How was your trip?" To them, such questions may feel hollow unless the person asking has a sincere interest and the capacity to listen to their authentic, complicated response. We take a closer look at re-entry in the next chapter.

Seven

Unpacking Your Bags

> And the world cannot be discovered by a journey of miles, no matter how long, but only by a spiritual journey, a journey of one inch, very arduous and humbling and joyful, by which we arrive at the ground at our feet, and learn to be at home.
>
> —Sarah York

The day arrives when the mission trip must end. Hopefully the experience was positive overall, and all participants have begun to experience some kind of transformation. On the trip, they quickly took on responsibilities and roles different from everyday life. For better or worse, living and working in a communal way presented an opportunity to learn about their own ability to adapt, perhaps to lead. They explored new relationships, new ways of seeing the world, and new paths for spiritual growth. Yet, the journey does not end when the mission team returns home. The group and its members will have much to unpack spiritually, socially, and emotionally, as well as logistically. Offer a follow-up process that will nurture the transformations they have begun.

The Challenges of Re-entry

The first order of business at home is to figure out how to *be* home. The power of a mission trip lies in traveling a distance of internal discovery and growth as well as of literal miles. Coming back also requires traveling a distance.

Anger, sadness, and numbness—whether or not they surfaced during the trip itself—almost always appear in the days and weeks following a trip as participants re-enter their daily routines. Some may carry lingering sadness or depression in response to a disheartening and/or unjust situation they have witnessed. Others may feel helpless, wishing they could have made a bigger difference. For some, new understandings of how our American society has contributed to injustice may engender anger, confusion, or apathy. Others may feel overwhelmed by the effort to integrate all they have experienced.

Youth team members have likely received financial and moral support from parents, caregivers, or the congregation. Yet when the team returns home, youth may act withdrawn, at odds, or reluctant to share stories about their experience. They may find it difficult, initially, to satisfy the needs of family and friends for reconnection. Sifting and sorting through the experiences of the trip is part of a normal re-entry process. Group leaders should use intentional strategies to minimize the isolation of team members from their families, peers who did not participate in the trip, the rest of the congregation, and friends. Support the youth, and their families and friends, as they wait it out.

Re-entry will energize some participants. Some immediately, and others once they have had time to process their experience, will be inspired to work for change with newfound purpose and meaning.

Debriefing

Gather the group for a debriefing session promptly on your arrival home. This will bring the trip experience full circle. Reviewing the nuts and bolts of the experience will help work out kinks in the logistics so a future trip will run more smoothly. Use a variety of creative approaches to draw out members' thoughts about what worked well, what could be improved, and possibilities for future mission projects.

One approach is to lead the group to revisit their own journal entries from the early stages of planning to now. Channel the energy of the team into brainstorming ideas and planning for future social justice work. You might offer the group one last journal prompt: What are my intentions for keeping social justice work at the center of my life as a Unitarian Universalist?

Where Do You Go from Here?

While the trip is fresh, plan a potluck meal or simply a meeting where participants can reconnect. Such a gathering will serve team members' need and desire to maintain the interpersonal connections they developed while away. Plan a way for families to participate in the retelling and shared understanding of the trip experience; this can ease families' reconnection.

Consider, as a group, where this trip may lead you. Continue to talk about the group's experience and invite participants to articulate their new understandings of a call to social justice. This will help extend the learning at home and support youth who are eager to continue the work and connect to other social action initiatives in your congregation and/or community. Lead the group to reflect: In what ways was the mission trip a self-contained experience? In what ways can it connect with or develop into something else?

Be realistic about your ability to support the group's ongoing interest. If your time and availability will be limited, connect the youth with others in your congregation who can help them sustain and channel their energy and enthusiasm.

Share Your Experience with the Congregation and Other Groups

A presentation to the congregation will gratify the staff, volunteers, and members who supported the trip with their time, money, mentorship, or other resources. Use this gathering to inspire others to do similar work in the future as well.

Find ways for participants to synthesize and share trip highlights in a way that conveys its meaning. Some ideas are:

- Work with the minister and/or Worship Committee to plan a service that shares some of your experiences.
- Collaborate with the Social Action Committee to present an informational forum that features slide shows.
- Network and build local partnerships and relationships to advance a justice issue, based on the group's learning from the trip.
- Accept invitations to have members of your group speak to other groups considering a mission trip or interested in the mission issues.

No matter which ways you choose to unpack the mission trip, it is unlikely that any participant will experience it as an isolated event, separate from the rest of their life. More likely, the trip will become part of their whole life's journey, a deep anchor and powerful fuel for ongoing exploration of ways to engage the world in right relation in your faith community, the local community, or distant lands.

Testimonial

And Thy Neighbor as Thyself

I am a born Universalist. Early on I became involved in the work of the Universalist Service Committee by placing my dimes in red cardboard stockings and baseballs to support the work of the Clara Barton and Eliot Joslin camps for diabetic children. Then it was giving to the work of the Universalist Service Committee in Africa, Germany, Birzeit College in the West Bank (Palestinian territories), and the Jordan School in Suffolk, Virginia. I was so turned on to the work of the Universalist Service Committee that in 1957 and 1958 I participated in a work camp in Jugendwerk Druhwald with refugee youth from East Berlin, Germany. In 1965, my wife, Joyce, and I led a group of eight teenagers to Suffolk, Virginia, site of the Jordan School, which we had both supported as children—working on the Head Start program there in its first year. These experiences led me to help advise the Unitarian Universalist Service Committee in the beginnings of the JustWorks and JustJourneys programs—getting those patrician UU hands dirty with the work of the world.

In April of 2002, I helped escort seventeen fourteen- and fifteen-year-olds from my congregation on a pilgrimage to Boston, Massachusetts. It was Earth Sunday, and a few from our group heard a passionate sermon on the moral imperative of vegetarianism. An accompanying father who heard that sermon—"Brad the Dad," we called him—a Xerox scientist, was impressed by its power, which so forcefully challenged the ethics of his own eating habits. Afterward he asked me, with ironic humor, "What is the half-life of a sermon?" The term *half-life* refers to the process by which a radioactive isotope falls to half its original power. This process continues ad infinitum, but the power of the isotope never really reaches zero. What is the half-life of matters spiritual? Ethical? I rather like the idea that these experiences of youth will have a lasting influence on them. It's what I call spiritual osmosis. Our souls have permeable membranes. Such sacred journeys influence us in ways we may never know.

In the summer of 1983, I took our older son, then sixteen, to the Women's Peace Encampment at Seneca Army Depot in upstate New York, reputed to be a neutron bomb storage site. Ever since attending the UU United Nations Youth Seminar that spring, he has been an activist. The scene was ominous. The police, with their flashing lights, and a growing knot of unfriendly townspeople formed a gauntlet between our parking space and the protestors. I could sniff violence in the wind. But when I said I thought we ought to leave, he asked me why and persuaded me to stay. We stayed to witness our values. That son served as president of Fourth Universalist Society in New York City and is still an activist.

In 1985, our younger son participated in a program created by three Denver-area churches. Eight UU youth lived with local families and were linked to community programs from the ACLU to Planned Parenthood, from soup kitchens to homeless shelters. Two weekly reflection periods with a UU seminarian provided opportunities for them to analyze their experience in the light of Unitarian Universalist values. So, take one sixteen-year-old from a white, liberal, and idealistic family and drop him into Denver's ghetto. Let him be an intake worker in a shelter for street people or have him dish up food in a soup kitchen. He learned, firsthand, something of what it takes to make the world even a tad better. He encountered some harsh social reality in a program sponsored by his religious community. In 1988, he interned with the Unitarian Universalist Peace Network in Philadelphia. He attended the University of Nairobi for his junior year of college, later working with a Kenyan hill farmer and taking his parents on an illuminating student's-eye view of that third world country. Now, as a middle school history teacher, he has his students engaged with settling new refugees, with Habitat for Humanity, and otherwise reflecting on the world into which they will soon move.

For years the Rochester Unitarian youth group served the soup kitchen at Blessed Sacrament Roman Catholic Church; they worked with Habitat for Humanity for a weekend, experiencing an urban ghetto firsthand. More recently, some of these youth went to the *maquiladoras* (factories) on the U.S.-Mexican border, with the New York State Labor and Religion Committee. They saw some of the results of the North American Free Trade Agreement. In each case, they had class-time opportunities for religious reflection. More recently, they and other youth groups have gone to the Gulf Coast to help with the rebuilding of communities in the wake of Hurricane Katrina. One youth, Brad the Dad's son, became a supervisor in a Catholic Worker soup kitchen and a leader in the peace movement, and spent six months volunteering at a home of homeless and street children in Asuncion, Paraguay. He graduated from high school in 2005. *The Rochester Catholic Worker* newsletter wished him well: "They are blessed to receive his energy and dedication as we have been."

Now, what religious values are embodied in these narratives?

Heresy Choosing to challenge conventional wisdom and entrenched power. I have come to the conclusion that, to raise children of good will, one must constantly question the prevailing cultural values. Our culture has become terribly self-indulgent. We must struggle to overcome the dominant narcissism and preserve the basic values of human service and social responsibility.

Cognitive dissonance Learning by exposure to a radically different environment. Students of human development tell us that basic values are formed in the decisive adolescent years. Without such experiences, children of affluence do not experience the clash of idealism and reality necessary to moral growth. Greed, once a vice, has become a virtue and infects us all. We need to serve not only children at risk of poverty but children at risk of affluence.

Empathy A "feeling with" the other, especially with the dispossessed of this world. We all need to have experiences that take us out of our comfort zones into contact with the "others" with whom we have little experience. In the class warfare of our society these experiences don't often come naturally; they need to be planned. Religious educators need to build on the natural empathy that is part of the package human nature grants us.

Stewardship Participation in a religious community that means something—that models love and peace and justice—in which the whole congregation is part of the teaching team. As historian Conrad Wright says, "Joining a church should not be the same as joining the National Geographic Society." We are not only individuals; we are members of a community. And as Ralph Waldo Emerson said, "No member of a crew is praised for the rugged individuality of his rowing."

Empowerment Education against feelings of helplessness. There is a Christian concept called equipping the saints, a way of saying that religiously motivated change agents need education and training to engage in peace and justice work. In a world where we are being outmaneuvered by a highly motivated and resource-rich religious right, we need to do more than casual preparation for social action.

Action Walking the talk in a world of paralysis by analysis. Every religious education program at every level ought to have a social action component. Our goal is to grow good neighbors who will understand that helping to repair the world is no extracurricular activity; it is simply part of what it is to be Unitarian Universalist.

This is praxis: learning by doing—the human dialogue of action and reflection. We need to "walk the talk," or embody our values, and "talk the walk," or become able to articulate why we do what we do. The experiences I have described are immensely enriched when participants have opportunities to put them in theological and ethical context. What we have here is "a church without walls." One of our tasks as religious educators/activists is to expand the Unitarian Universalist horizon beyond the confines of a religious institution. All of this is in the context of a teaching, learning, lifespan religious community. The church teaches by what it is and does.

Unitarian Universalist folk singer Pete Seeger has been a public nuisance for a long time. He has sung, strummed, and spoken for peace and justice. He once built a schooner called Clearwater to take people on Hudson River excursions and enlist their support for cleaning up the river. Although it was a small endeavor, Seeger likened it to a seesaw with one end anchored to the ground by a basket of rocks, while activists were at the other end using teaspoons to slowly fill a basket with sand. Some day the balance will tip and the rocks will be sent flying into the air. People will ask, "How did that happen so quickly?" It was because of "us and our damned little teaspoons." These sacred journeys to be with the neighbor provide our youth, and us, with the opportunity to get busy with our teaspoons.

RICHARD S. GILBERT, a retired Unitarian Universalist minister, is the author of *Building Your Own Theology* (Boston: Unitarian Universalist Association), *The Prophetic Imperative: Social Gospel in Theory and Practice* (Boston: Skinner House Books), and other works.

Testimonial

Connecting Souls on a Navajo Reservation

Cars traveling along the highway to Montezuma Creek slowed and stared as they passed a contingent of cyclists making the long trip across the Utah desert. Exhausted, hot, thirsty, and covered with a mixture of sweat and fine, red dirt, this group of young people continued onward. There was a baseball field that needed fixing.

This describes the high school youth of the Unitarian Church of Harrisburg (UCH), Pennsylvania, in partnership with youth of the Navajo Nation, as they took part in a two-week spiritual quest—a quest designed to stretch the body and mind and grow the soul. For this trip, we joined hands with Navajo Youth Empowerment Services to spend two weeks biking across the Navajo Reservation, alongside Navajo youth, completing service projects along the way. Thirteen youth and two adult advisors chose to leave their comfort zones to experience the joy of service, the thrill of discovering another culture, and the loving support of a youth group bound by a common mission.

This journey did not begin when we got on the plane to fly to New Mexico. The journey began more than a year prior to our departure, when we began planning for the trip. The UCH high school youth group was growing rapidly. Our regular youth group activities of learning, social action, leadership, and intergenerational church involvement were flourishing with high attendance and high enthusiasm. The leadership of the group felt it was the right time for the group to take the next step in growth. What experience would deepen their UU roots as they matured into young adults? We knew that the Boston heritage trip for the Coming of Age youth created a strong group bond and enhanced the sense of Unitarian Universalist identity. How could that be duplicated for high school-age youth?

Unitarian Universalism calls us to act when we see injustice, not just talk about it. The seven Principles resonate most when UUs are engaged in meaningful service projects, working and growing alongside those they wish to serve. A trip for high school youth that had service as its focus would nurture a love of social action while also creating deeper friendships among the youth. The decision was made to add a service trip for high school youth to the church programming. Youth, parents, and advisors researched viable service trips, and youth then took a vote. The group decided to partner with Navajo Youth Empowerment Services (Navajo Y.E.S.), an organization that provides outdoor adventure activities for Navajo youth while teaching the value of a drug-free lifestyle. In a leap of faith, Navajo Y.E.S. agreed to have us join them during a segment of their Tour de Rez, a summer-long bike relay during which Navajo youth learn about the nation in which they live, while also completing service projects. In return, the UCH youth group spent more than a year raising more than $5,000 over the money we would spend on personal travel expenses, to donate to Navajo Y.E.S.

In addition to fundraising and completing training miles on bikes, the youth group spent time learning about the Navajo culture during the months before the trip. We read Navajo creation stories, participated in a cultural workshop led by a local Native American, planned and led a Navajo-themed worship service for the congregation, and taught a class for the younger UUs about Navajo sand paintings. We tried our hand at making fry bread and talked about cultural taboos to avoid while on the trip. Each participant started keeping a journal; before departure, youth reflected on topics such as their stereotypes of Native Americans and their personal growth goals for the trip.

Finally we traveled by plane and crowded van to the Four Corners region of the reservation, where we joined with a group of

Navajo youth who had been on this venture for weeks already. The itinerary was rigorous. Altogether, we biked almost one hundred miles, hiked several more on top of that, and even rafted part of the way down the San Juan River. Along the route, we stopped to complete service projects. We performed trail maintenance on a path leading to a gorgeous 110-foot waterfall. We repaired a run-down baseball field at a local elementary school. We dug an irrigation ditch to direct spring water to a cluster of fruit trees on a traditional Navajo farm. The willingness of the Navajo people to include us in their journey created the opportunity for our youth to experience a different culture firsthand. Through games of cards, shared meals, common struggles on tiring days, and even a shared worship experience, the Navajo and Harrisburg youth created a bond that reached across a large cultural gap. As one youth said in her journal, "Even though they live on a reservation across the country and don't know who Chuck Norris is, we are similar people, capable of being great companions."

Journal writings were part of a daily ritual for our group. Every evening before bedtime, we gathered to reflect on highlights and struggles of the day. This intentional contemplation added to group unity and allowed participants to process the onslaught of feelings that emerged during this challenging trip. Here are some excerpts:

> "The big lesson I took away was the feeling of compassion. Tired, sore, and sweaty, everyone could have easily given up. Yet we knew that there were things more important than material items: each other. We supported each other. If someone was falling back, we'd encourage them, carry things for them. People were understanding and willing to do anything possible to paint a smile on your face."

> "It's about love. Love for the people you will never know, and for the people you will always keep close to you."

> "I kicked butt on that 41.5-mile ride, which is way more than I ever thought I could do. I've already amazed myself.

> I can do anything, and I don't have anything to prove to anyone anymore."
>
> "I've honestly become more aware of what is essential, and what is a 'want.'"
>
> "Most importantly, I have learned lessons in diversity and how the 'process' of acceptance is much more challenging than the 'philosophy' of acceptance."

Because of the success of this trip, the high school youth planned to participate in a service trip each summer. In July 2009, the group spent a week in Washington D.C. at a service learning hostel called the Pilgrimage. The programming for the week included an ambitious list of service projects, during which the group witnessed urban homelessness for what it is. In combination with these projects, the schedule included interactive workshops. In one such workshop called "The Basics of Life," participants were led on an imaginary trip into the downward spiral of poverty. Step by step, participants and their families were led through the difficulties of living in poverty as "the basics of life" are stripped away one by one. Groups were then asked to reflect on the most important and most expendable aspects of their lives.

During another workshop, at the end of the week, youth worked with the Pilgrimage poet-in-residence (a man who has experienced homelessness firsthand) to write poetry describing their experiences during the week. The intentional inclusion of interactive workshops made this trip more meaningful than just serving food and picking up trash. The educational component compelled us to reflect on how our Unitarian Universalist faith calls us to work for those in desperate situations. The hope is that the youth will carry the face of the homeless with them wherever they go.

A successful service trip does not end upon returning home. The effects of the trip will follow participants throughout their lives. After the trip to the Navajo Reservation, the youth created a display for the congregation to view during coffee hour one Sunday morning. A parent created a DVD of many pictures from the trip which played along with some inspiring Native American music. A senior youth created a display board highlighting the three service projects that were completed. All youth submitted journal entries that were typed and displayed around the room. The response from the congregation was amazing. They had encouraged us along the way with words of commendation and financial support, through our fundraisers. Showing them a piece of what we had experienced was an essential component of the trip.

In addition to returning with lots of stories and pictures, we returned with different souls. During our days in the Southwest desert, the soul of our youth group grew more cohesive, the souls of the youth felt the value of service, and the soul of the Navajo became connected to the soul of the UU in central Pennsylvania.

WENDY SHAVER is the youth director for the Unitarian Church of Harrisburg, Pennsylvania.

When Dreams Become Action

My friend once said that she was going to be somebody someday. "But aren't you already somebody?" I asked. "No," she said, "I mean somebody who does something *for* somebody that changes their life." I thought that goal was one I, too, wanted to accomplish.

After coming home from Mississippi, I felt like I had achieved that goal. I felt so proud that I had been part of something that made someone's life better. So proud that I had put my heart, soul, blood, and sweat into that common goal. The people we helped probably don't remember my name—I don't even recall telling them—and they probably don't even remember what I did. But I do, and my friends do, and that is enough for me. Even if the people I helped forget me and what I did, I won't care: My name may not remain, but my work will.

To be part of something so huge is hard to describe. To look around in the morning at a car full of people who cared, who wanted to help, made an aura that was incredible. To see the effects of our work, how our work paid off, meant more to me than probably almost anything I have ever done.

Going to Mississippi was probably one of the smartest choices I made. It taught me so much. It taught me what hard work really is (I will never look at vacuuming the same way) and how all that hard work pays off. It put in perspective how little my problems are. Who cares if you want to win a science fair compared to someone who lost their home, belongings, and pretty much everything else? But it also showed me how people working together toward a common goal can achieve so much and give somebody a home back. Seeing the joy on those people's faces when they saw their completed house was unbelievable and unforgettable. One guy named Buster told us his story, and he started to cry when he began talking about how his life could now move on from Katrina, because of us and our help.

Dreams will take you far, but actions will go farther. You can dream all you want of having a new home after it was destroyed in Katrina, but the action of rebuilding that person's house will take that dream farther. It will take that dream into reality.

The Mississippi trip opened my eyes to so many things. I went there worried about the people, but I learned there were more than people grieving. I knew animals had been cast out, killed, and hurt during Katrina. A few good souls tried to take in as many animals as they could, but with the overpowering numbers, the individual animals were practically starving.

Don't make the assumptions I made. I thought these people were cruel and mistreated animals, but conversations with one family showed the very opposite. The people loved their animals, but were overwhelmed trying to take care of ten horses, fifteen dogs, kittens, and themselves.

We banded together and collected around $130. We bought feed, brushes, medicine, bowls, anything we thought would help. When we delivered this to the people, I felt something I had felt before, but not in this magnitude. I felt the joy of knowing that I had done far more than was required of me. It was amazing.

While the emotional part of this trip was extremely draining, we let loose several times. We made a mini-tradition of going to the beach after work to unwind. Watching my friends run from swarming, evil jellyfish brought tears of laughter to my eyes. We dyed our hair purple. It was supposed to wash out, but my friend Henry is still asked if he dyed his hair. We goofed off to relieve the stress.

I will take these memories and stories with me forever. I also think I am still taking some bug bites! Despite all the emotional and physical demands, I would never trade this experience, these memories, and the lifelong bonds I have made, for anything.

Like the song says, dreams can take you very far, but actions will take you farther.

I am somebody.

MaKensie Schumaker offered these reflections in spring 2008, following a youth mission trip, in a homily to the Greenville UU Fellowship in South Carolina.

Testimonial

From Before to After

The day before we left our suburban Boston church basement and headed out on our first week-long service trip to Paterson, New Jersey, I handed out a little questionnaire to the sixteen giddy members of our youth group, who thought they'd come only to pick up a packing list and some pizza.

Questionnaire: WHY I AM GOING ON THIS SERVICE TRIP
Please rank the following, with 1 being the number one reason you signed up to go on this trip and 6 being the very last reason you are going.

_____ Because my friends are.
_____ I really want to help people.
_____ I love power tools.
I want to learn something I can't learn in school and do different, meaningful work.
_____ I need this for my college applications.
_____ I want to go grow as a person and challenge myself in new ways.

Prior to this, we'd met for weeks to do fundraising, to talk about homelessness, to review the demographics of Paterson, to ask questions about what it means to "serve," and to participate in antiracism and anti-oppression workshops—planning meetings that were necessary, in my mind, not just for educational reasons but also to build a sense of responsibility, gratitude, and teamwork before we tackled a challenging week.

In spite of all my efforts to educate them prior to the experience, the last-minute questionnaire revealed that four of the youth were going because they loved power tools; six had checked "because my friends are" as their number one reason for going; and five had chosen "I need this for my college applications" as one of their top three reasons for going. Only one wanted to "help people," as his number two reason, and not one youth, apparently, was doing this to learn anything, do anything meaningful, or be challenged in any new way. Hoping that perhaps some had signed up for this trip for a reason I hadn't thought of, I'd asked them if any had another reason for going. One youth did: "It's something to do," he shrugged.

Over the course of that week in Paterson, we worked with Melissa, her husband, and their two older children to finish framing what would be their very first home; we dug out a foundation for another house with Mike and several long-term Habitat volunteers; and we finished painting another house in the same vicinity for a couple who were eager to move into their new home so they could move out of their car before the winter set in. We shared lunches with the future homeowners and children in the neighborhood, eating quickly with grimy hands, out of the backs of our vans, so we could get back to our jobs; and we stayed up too late after every nine-hour workday, talking about the people we had met and grown to love and trading stories we'd been told or overheard. Occasionally, after we took cold two-minute showers, shopped for food, and made and ate dinner together, we sorted donated clothing for the thrift shop where we were staying. Its owners had allowed us to camp out in their building without even knowing who we were, assuming that if we were good enough to devote our vacation week to building homes with Habitat, then we must be good enough to take care of their space.

A week after that trip, as we sat once again in the basement of our church, I asked the same group of youth, "What are you going to tell your friends about your vacation week working in Paterson?" They wrote the following:

"I truly believe that I have been touched, a light inside of me has been relit. I am a changed person and have a renewed amount of strength to deal with my own troubles, and I want to work to help others with theirs from now on. That's all I'm going to say."

—KENDRA, A SOPHOMORE, CAPTAIN OF THE SKI TEAM, TENNIS PLAYER, AND POET

"I won't even try to describe it. It changed me at some deep level. I was happier last week than I have been for a long, long time now, even though I was filthy and blistered and exhausted."

—ETHAN, A JUNIOR WHO LOVED ALL THINGS MILITARY

"I wouldn't say this has changed me into a totally new person, but this trip *did* change me. The whole idea of building a community together with our hands and our tools is so amazing. And seeing the effect our kindness had on Mike and Sarah and Heidi was even more amazing. I feel like I've grown so much emotionally and spiritually. I don't know how I could describe the effect an experience like this can have on a group of kids our age. I feel confident that, for many of us, this is only the beginning of a life devoted to compassion and justice."

—ANDREW, A JUNIOR SINGER AND SONGWRITER

"I'd say that this trip has been one of the greatest experiences of my life. It has really made me think about who I am and who I want to be. I have always had trouble thinking about what I want to do with my life, but this trip is making me contemplate new things, like joining AmeriCorps, or at least continuing to volunteer with Habitat."

—KELLY, A SENIOR WHO WENT ON TO JOIN AMERICORPS

"I was talking to my friend last night, and he said that he wouldn't mind doing this sort of work well into old age. And you know, I have to agree with him. I haven't felt this happy or useful *ever*. It wasn't only the thrill of pounding nails or the satisfaction of shoveling my whole pile of dirt or getting to know the family who was moving in, but just knowing that we were making a difference in someone's life. I cried the last day, leaving the work site. I haven't cried in *years*."

—MARK, A JUNIOR WRITER AND FILMMAKER

"This is the only time in my life that I've seen such a diverse group of people come together to accomplish something significant, and it happened in just one week. I know that even though our work was meaningful, it also didn't make a huge dent in the problem. I think the week was more symbolic of what is possible for and of people."

—KATHY, A SENIOR BALLERINA

"I'm not saying I'm perfect, but I think I'm a better person because of this, with a more clearly defined direction for my life. I hope we all find a way to incorporate the 'lessons learned' into our daily lives and our futures. We owe it to ourselves and everyone we met and everyone who paid for us to go on this trip to make sure that it has more than a week's worth of impact on our lives and on the world."

—MOLLY, A FRESHMAN WHO WENT ON TO ORGANIZE MORE THAN FIFTY SERVICE TRIPS AT HER COLLEGE

In the wake of their responses to my questions before and after that first service trip, I never doubted that faith development took place during service work. I just wanted to figure out how to make every service trip as transformative as this one had been.

For more than a decade now, our youth group, which has grown from sixteen to more than sixty members (many of whom have been drawn to the group because of our community service), has spent winter and spring vacation weeks building houses in inner cities, farming on Native American reservations, cleaning up after natural disasters, and organizing and staffing day camps for kids whose parents couldn't be home with them over their school break. Over the course of these service trips, some dramatic in their effect, some subtle, we've figured out the elements that make for a meaningful weeklong experience—and laid a strong foundation for lifelong faith development.

When planning our trips now, we seek out opportunities for authentic service, finding that our youth need to do work that meets a real need, not work that merely attempts to keep them busy and make them feel useful—and they always know the difference. We stress to the youth that authentic service also means listening and responding to the needs and desires of those they are serving, rather than doing tasks that appeal to them. Once, we went to a Habitat for Humanity site prepared to build a house—and ended up building nothing more than doorframes and sawhorses for a week, because that was what was needed. After a few days of grousing and one serious evening discussion about "edifice complexes," our service-trip motto was born: "It's not about you."

The work trips that developed and nurtured the youth's sense of self and interconnectedness—not just among themselves but also in the larger community—were those weeks during which youth formed reciprocal relationships with the people they were serving. Youth need to work with, not just for, those in need, so we search for service trips that allow the greatest amount of personal contact between the youth and those who will benefit from their work. Similarly, raising money or sending supplies doesn't engage teenagers in a way that is powerful enough to be life-transforming unless they have already had the opportunity to know, identify with, and care about some of the people they're helping. More than anything else, firsthand encounters with those in need are the experiences that lead young people to ask important questions about economic and racial disparities in this country and the world—and about their own responsibility for changing them.

For that same reason, we now engage ourselves in projects that we can continue from year to year, returning to the same places or people we've helped and met in prior trips. While our choice to do so was not initially as well received as service trips that took us to exciting new destinations every year, our youth now understand and are willing to trade the thrill of venturing to new places for a longer-term investment in particular people and communities. "Now," one sophomore said, "we're more focused on working and relationships than we are on going on trips, and that's how it should be."

As leaders, we have honed our own skills to ensure that our evening discussions throughout the service weeks lead the youth to reflect on the meaning of their service experiences from a religious perspective. Youth need to be skillfully guided to reflect on the meaning of their day's work in a way that fosters intentional and positive faith development as UUs, or we run the risk of merely providing them with an emotionally charged but isolated experience. One youth group alum who is currently involved in service work through her university noted differences between her college service experiences and those with our church youth group. She contrasted the two kinds of trips by describing her university service trips this way: "Everyone just sort of works hard, gets done whatever we're doing, and doesn't think about it at all. And neither the people in charge nor the participants worry much about why we chose that particular service to do; why that particular thing was a good use of our time; whether we worked effectively; what we learned from it (if anything); or why it was important for us or for the people we served." Nightly discussions during our service trips are mandatory, are both leader- and youth-led, and focus as much on what we are receiving as on what we are giving—but we are there to help others. Building our carpentry skills or our resumes or our better selves are by-products, albeit great ones, of our trips, but they are not our goal.

We suggest to the youth, even before presenting them with the opportunity to participate in our service trips, that their faith as a UU is a way of living—a set of behaviors and habits, not just an adherence to a code of beliefs. And we reiterate throughout the week that faith, while it might begin with one act (or one week), is a lifelong process; practicing their faith means, among other things, continuing to give of their time and talent and resources to help others in need, engaging in justice work, bearing some responsibility for the wrongs they see in the world, and caring not just for a week but for a lifetime. Long after our trips are done, we continue our work—by collecting and sending things people have asked for, by educating others about the situation we encountered, and by making plans to return the following year. Many of our youth carry on their commitment to service and justice long after their high school and college years.

Six months after Hurricane Katrina hit, thirty-three youth, five adults, and two of our youth group alums made the first of sixteen congregational, intergenerational work trips to the Gulf Coast. At our first preparatory meeting, I thought it might be interesting to give the youth the trusty "reasons for going" questionnaire again.

"Are you joking?" one of them said, staring at the sheet.

"This is dumb," another muttered.

"What do you mean?" I asked. "Just fill it out."

Silence.

Finally, another offered, "I mean . . . we *can't*. I mean, people don't have *homes*. We have to *do something*. There isn't any reason or any five reasons—or whatever—for doing it; it's just what you have to *do*. It's what *we* do."

And there it was, faith development in action. Our community service, once just a thing to do, had become the thing *we* do.

JESSICA RUBENSTEIN is director of youth ministries at the Winchester Unitarian Society in Massachusetts.

Testimonial

There We Were, Standing on Top of the World

Transformation. We were warned about it, but I don't think many of us listened. I mean, I am who I am. I'm already a good person. There are poor people. I get it. But on Tuesday, February 20, at approximately 5:30 p.m. Mountain Time, I realized for myself that I don't get it and I probably never will. The sun setting, a chill was washing over the barren landscape of Anapra, Mexico. Our mission team was finishing its second day of building and, in the rapidly deepening world of blue, it was time to start clean-up.

We were gathering tools and scraps of wood and depositing them in the truck as children scurried around playing and helping. One boy, an eight-year-old named Jorge, approached me. He beckoned me to follow him. I did my best to express in Spanish that I would have to work now, but maybe tomorrow. Jorge wouldn't take no for an answer. Grabbing my hand, he pulled me with surprising force to the hill that the house backed up against, and proceeded to lead me up.

He scurried quickly to the top of the hill and I followed, seconds behind him. The wind picked up and the air took on a fresher, cleaner smell. The sounds of the group below us faded into the rapidly thickening blue of night. There we were, me and Jorge, standing on top of the world.

Neither of us said anything for a long time, each of us gazing into the distance, taking in the landscape. I took off my red work bandana and let the wind whip through my hair. Standing at the top of that hill, I felt absolutely without a care. It wasn't me and some little Mexican kid standing on top of a hill. It was my friend Jorge and me, standing on top of the world itself.

Seconds passed in silence, and what I began to feel was both wonderful and terrifying at the same time. It was like the deepest part of my soul was being pushed down, dug out, and expanded to hold a whole new range of feelings and emotions. My stomach turned over and from the depths of my heart rose what, for me, was a new emotion; an emotion that felt like neither love nor pity.

I felt the muscles deep in my face, behind my eyes, tensing, preparing to let out my emotions. My heart and brain had come to the agreement that it was time for me to cry, and it seemed like there was nothing I could do to stop it. But before I could shed a single tear, Jorge was tugging on my sleeve. He motioned to suggest we go back down the hill and I followed him. Walking down the hill, I found myself in an emotional limbo. I was not sad and I was not happy. I was not peaceful and I was not disturbed. You know you're getting somewhere when you can't put your emotion in your emotions box. For the life of me, I could not put a finger on what I was feeling, which is unusual for me.

All of us were changed in one way or another on the mission trip. I cannot quite articulate what that change was or how it happened. In reality, the whole trip was a transformative process. Climbing the hill with Jorge was the first time it really occurred to me that I might possibly go home from Mexico different from when I came.

To be perfectly honest, I went into this experience with a lousy attitude—somewhere along the lines of "at worst, this is gonna be one long and very smelly college essay topic." But on the other side of the mission trip, it served to open my eyes to a lot of things: to injustice in the world, to the atrocities that our country perpetrates every day, to the ultimate good nature of humankind, and to a universal language of children. As important as all of that sounds, opening my eyes was only the beginning of the transformation. The real transformation was opening my heart.

Charlie Emple wrote this reflection in 2007 for a worship service at the Unitarian Universalist Church of Greater Lynn, Massachusetts.

Launching a Trip

Launching a trip on organized, practical footing creates the solid foundation for a powerful community experience. The resources in this section represent the first concrete steps to turn your idea of taking a mission trip into a reality.

The Organizational Fact Sheet offers questions to help you assess whether an organization is a good match for your group. For example, many organizations lead fabulous mission trips, yet at prohibitive cost. Also, there are more faith-based organizations than secular groups leading mission trips; discerning whether their work is compatible with Unitarian Universalist sensibilities is important.

The Trip Fact Sheet helps you compile information to help families evaluate whether their youth will participate in the trip. You will need to convey which elements are fixed and which are estimated or could change.

After you identify the team, pay the deposits, and make necessary preliminary reservations, hold your first team meeting to begin building a shared vision for the mission trip. Use the Visioning Session as a framework for a one-hour visioning workshop to ground the experience in faith from the beginning.

The Sample Itinerary offers a grid to illustrate how much work, learning, recreation, and relaxation will occur on the trip. Each mission trip will have its unique features, but in our experience, most have a rigorous line-up of daily activities. Specifically, several consecutive days of physical labor may be a new experience for some participants. A sample itinerary will prepare them for this possibility and increase their likelihood of meeting the challenge.

Find tools for assessing and meeting the team's financial need, beginning with the Sacred Dollars Covenant form on page 86. A sample group covenant (page 92) and Trip Expectations and Rules contract (page 95) will help your group develop your own versions of these important documents. The Team-Building Games resource (page 97) is followed by the Five Steps of Community Building document (page 99), widely used by Unitarian Universalist youth leadership groups.

Finally, review the Spiritual Preparation resource on page 104. Use the guide questions to shape your spiritual leadership before, during, and after the trip to prepare youth for and nurture them in the deep transformation your mission experience can generate.

Organizations That Work with Mission Teams

Many organizations do mission work. We are familiar with some from direct experience and others by referral. The list below offers a starting point for your search—it is by no means comprehensive. While many groups have had positive experiences working with these organizations, your mission team leaders are responsible for communicating with the chosen provider to understand the particular terms of your partnership. Be clear about mutual expectations, including the advance preparation the organization expects your team to do.

Annunciation House

Mission

Annunciation House is a Catholic organization that welcomes all faiths and operates houses of hospitality for migrants and refugees in the border region of El Paso, Texas, and Ciudad Juarez, Mexico. The resident volunteers assist migrant, homeless, and economically vulnerable peoples of the border region by providing hospitality, advocacy, and education. Border Awareness Experiences facilitates face-to-face meetings and encounters between participants, people, and groups on both sides of the border. Through these programs, Annunciation House aims to raise consciousness about issues facing the border region, such as immigration, economic development, human rights, and social justice.

Work
Border Awareness Experiences can vary in the number of days that each experience lasts. A typical itinerary includes visiting the U.S. Border Patrol, listening to the stories of migrants and refugees, touring a *maquiladora,* meeting human rights activists, and staying in a migrant shelter.

Website
http://annunciationhouse.org

Common Hope

Mission
Common Hope promotes hope and opportunity in Guatemala, partnering with children, families, and communities who want to participate in a process of development to improve their lives through education, health care, and housing.

Work
Eight- to ten-day Vision Team trips encounter a variety of work and learning activities that might include visiting families with a social worker, attending informal talks and discussions with staff members, sorting supplies in the warehouse, shelving books in the library, or possibly building a house or planting trees.

Website
www.commonhope.org

Gulf Coast Volunteers for the Long Haul

Mission
Gulf Coast Volunteers for the Long Haul helps people rebuild their homes, neighborhoods, communities, and lives in the aftermath of Hurricane Katrina. Started by the Winchester Unitarian Society, the project is committed to work "as long as it takes." Unitarian Universalist minister Mary J. Harrington serves as the organization's president.

Work
Week-long relief and recovery trips to the New Orleans area to rebuild and paint (homes, schools, and playgrounds), tutor elementary students, care for rescued pets, and listen to residents in neighborhoods that were severely damaged.

Web
www.longhaulvolunteers.org/index

Habitat for Humanity

Mission
Habitat for Humanity seeks to eliminate poverty housing and homelessness from the world and to make decent shelter a matter of conscience and action.

Work
Build houses in partnership with families in need in U.S. or international communities.

Website
www.habitat.org

Peace House

Mission
Peace House maintains two centers in Mexico, one in Chiapas and the other in Oaxaca, responding to a call for international solidarity with grassroots indigenous and *campesino* (farmer) movements. The organization seeks to further social justice and sustainable development in Mexico and the U.S. through education, network building, and facilitating firsthand experience of globalization and human rights issues.

Work
At this writing, the Peace House center in Oaxaca has a volunteer program.

Website
http://www.casacollective.org

Safe Passage

Mission
Safe Passage provides safe refuge and educational and nutritional support for children whose families scavenge the Guatemala City garbage dump as a means of survival.

Work
Volunteers provide classroom support and enrichment activities for the children, while bearing witness to the extreme poverty affecting these children and learning about the social and political root causes.

Website
www.safepassage.org

Unitarian Universalist Service Committee: JustWorks Camps

Mission
JustWorks camps, a project of the Unitarian Universalist Service Committee, are short-term projects that help volunteers examine and understand the causes and damaging effects of injustice. Participants work directly with people in the communities they serve, experiencing social justice struggles firsthand.

Work
Varies.

Website
http://www.uusc.org

Organization Fact Sheet

Organization: ______________________________

Telephone: ______________________________

Address/Website: ______________________________

Contact person: ______________________________

Email: ______________________________

What kind of work does the organization do?

____

Is it a faith-based organization?___ Yes___No

Does it work with faith-based mission teams?___ Yes___No

Is group size-limited?___ Yes___No

Are there age limitations?___ Yes___No

When can the organization accommodate your group?

____

Where is the project located in relation to the airport or port of entry?

____

In what kind of work would the team be involved?

______

What are the requirements for a youth-to-adult ratio?

______

Would your group be working or housed with other groups?

______

What special skills are participants required to have?

______

Does the organization provide leadership beforehand? On site?

______

What special considerations are there?

______

Contact information for referrals

______

What are the costs?

	per person	per group	paid to organization, or to another entity	payment due when?
Program fee				
Accommodations				
Meals				
Transportation				
Entertainment				
Other				

What is the cancellation policy?

______

RESOURCE

Trip Fact Sheet

Organization: ____________________

Mission of organization: ____________________

Location: ____________________

Group size: ____________________

What kind of work will the mission team member do each day?

____

What are the estimated costs of the trip?

	per person	group	
Travel (auto/air/bus/train)			
Passport and visa			
Local transportation			
Travel insurance			
Gas, tolls			
Accommodations			
Meals			
Supplies			
Program fee			
Discretionary			

Total Cost: ____________________

(For discretionary costs, calculate how much spending money participants will need. Suggest that all participants bring the same amount of discretionary money—an amount that is in keeping with a mission experience.)

Why are we doing this?

____

What will be challenging?

____

What will be rewarding?

____

How will we pay for the trip? How much will come from families, the congregation, another sponsor, additional fundraising?

____

What are the accommodations like?

____

What is the trip itinerary, beyond our stay at the base location?

____

What preparations do we need to ensure our health and safety on the trip (e.g., potable water, immunizations, emergency medical care)?

____

Why have we chosen this organization?

____

Visioning Session

After you have identified the team, paid the deposits, and made necessary preliminary reservations, your first team meeting is the time to begin building a shared vision for the experience. This framework for a one-hour visioning session can help ground the process in faith, from the beginning.

Chalice lighting

Reading

Welcome

Check-in

Invite participants to introduce themselves and each share one thing they want the group to know about them.

Discussion

Record responses to these questions for reference now and to revisit later.

- Why do you want to go on a mission trip?
- What are you looking forward to on this mission trip?
- What concerns do you have?
- What are you curious about?

Check-out

Prompt participants to say one word about how they feel about being part of this mission team. Or, offer a check-out question for each person to answer.

Reflection/Closing

Reflect back to the group highlights of what individuals shared. Acknowledge there will be much to look forward to and that individuals' concerns will be addressed in the months ahead.

Extinguishing the chalice

Choose an appropriate reading to close the session.

Sample Itinerary

Day/ Date	Time/ Location	Activity	Must bring
Day 1	10 am	Meet at airport	Yourself, luggage, ID
Day 2			
Day 3			
Day 4			
Day 5			
Day 6			
Day 7			

RESOURCE

Sacred Dollars Covenant

There are a variety of ways to determine the amount of scholarship assistance, or sacred dollars, needed for a particular mission trip. One approach that ensures anyone can participate in the trip, regardless of financial need, requires that participants (and their parents or caretakers) confidentially state the amount they can each afford to pay toward the total cost of the trip. The group leader or adult advisor calculates the difference between the total trip cost and the amount each family can afford. That total, plus the donation amount the team is required to pay or wants to provide the organization, becomes the team's fundraising goal.

This approach acknowledges that each participant has different financial needs (e.g., perhaps some participants can afford their entire expense, others need a significant subsidy, and still others fall somewhere in between). Addressing the financial needs of the group as a team challenge is crucial. You will set the expectation that the team will take care of its members and acknowledge the reality of unequal distribution of wealth and resources, an issue that is a centerpiece of mission work. Here is a template to use for this approach:

Youth Name:

I understand that the estimated trip cost is $____ per person (including airfare). I am committing to paying *this amount* toward *my* trip cost: $____.

I understand that I am expected to fully participate in team fundraising, and if fundraising goals are not met, I will be expected to explore ways to help the group raise the balance.

Signature: ____

Parent Signature: ____________________________________

Date: ____

**This form must be received by ____________ [group leader or adult advisor] by ____________ [date], along with a deposit of $ ____________ .

Resource

Fundraising Worksheet

This worksheet will help you organize any fundraising event you host—whether you are raising funds to support the scholarship needs of your group, the host organization, or both.

There are no magic formulas for identifying the best event. However, you can maximize your success and ensure more enjoyment for the group if you focus on activities that capture the interests and creative talents of group members. Whether you choose a car wash, bake sale, community supper, dance, talent show, guest speakers, auction, or concert, be sure to consider how you will infuse the event with education about your mission trip and the good work the group is about to do.

[Name of Fundraising Event]	who	when	cost	notes
Event coordinator				
Administration				
Before the event:				
Publicity/advertising				
Shopping				
During the event:				
Cooking				
Serving				
Set up				
Decorations/display				
Breakdown/cleanup				
Collecting money/tickets				
Refreshments				
Supplies for Event				
Custodial coverage				
[Ticket price] x [number of tickets that will be sold] = [projected income from ticket sales]				
Other income				
Total costs of the event				
Anticipated Profit				

Fundraising Letter

A well-crafted fundraising letter is an effective way to broaden the base of financial support to include team members' friends and family who live elsewhere and are unable to participate in local fundraisers. The process of writing a fundraising letter will help group members articulate the reason(s) they chose to participate in the mission trip. The letter itself can educate others about the work the team will be doing. If you choose to do this activity, encourage all group members to participate, whether or not they are seeking scholarship assistance for themselves. Part of working together as a team includes ensuring that everyone who wants to participate in the mission trip is able to, regardless of need.

Provide these content guidelines to team members:

- Explain why you are writing this letter and why you are asking for your friend's or relative's support. Include where you are going, when you are going, information about the group or organization, and a brief description of the work you will do.
- Be sure to include why you are fundraising: Are you raising money to support the scholarship needs of the group and/or to support the organization you will be working with?
- Explain why you are excited about participating in this mission trip, or why you think mission work is important, and how you think your friend's or relative's donation will help you or the group you are supporting.
- Ask the donor to send their tax-deductible donation to your congregation's mailing address.

- Ask the donor to make the check payable to your congregation and to include your name on the memo line. (This will facilitate the ability to track donations so group members can thank donors who make contributions on their behalf.) If your congregation can accept electronic or credit card payments, include that information as well.
- Explain how letter recipients can access a blog that you or the group have, or will have, to keep others updated while you are on the mission trip.
- Thank letter recipients for their support.

Instruct team members to show their letters to a group leader or adult advisor for approval before they mail them. The leader or advisor should check the letters for accuracy, particularly the information about the organization or group you will be working with and the process the letter describes for making contributions.

Covenanting

At the core of our Unitarian Universalist faith is our spiritual and communal practice of covenanting. At all stages of a mission trip—planning, doing, and whatever comes after—the practice of covenanting is vital to defining, guiding, and embedding the experience as a significant life event. Because this guidebook focuses on youth, there are particular requirements to ensure the physical, emotional, and spiritual well-being of minors.

Youth groups and events commonly have a standard set of rules that are used widely in our Association and are upheld in the peer culture. They include:

- no exclusive behavior
- no sexualized activity
- no drugs or alcohol
- no weapons
- no pets
- no leaving the grounds
- zero tolerance for violence and abuse.

Although these seem like commonsense rules, any adult who assumes responsibility for minors should fully understand that the rules provide critical safety for the group, and should commit to uphold them. Exclusive behavior, in particular, can happen spontaneously; without proper attention, it can skew the group dynamic. Inform youth that on the mission trip, they will have fewer freedoms than they are used to having in their home environments. It takes wise and strong adult leaders to persist in this strict groundwork, which will create the group's capacity for the transformative experience they are about to have.

In addition to the rules, the group will need a covenant. As important as the requirements to obtain a passport or inoculations for out-of-country travel is the requirement that the group prepare spiritually to travel together. Youth, as well as some adults, may suggest that an implied, common group understanding of mutual care and respect is all they need. Our research and direct experience tell us, however, that a group should not cut corners by diminishing the importance of a covenant.

Creating a covenant for a mission trip affirms team-building leading up to the trip. It produces a contract which spells out, for everyone, the parameters for joining the trip, and gives the group a touchstone to use while traveling together.

Share these questions in a large group gathering, in small groups, or as journal prompts to guide a process of creating a trip covenant:

- What made you decide to participate in this mission trip?
- How do you think the trip will change you, if at all?
- What is your vision for this trip?
- How will you know the trip was successful?
- What concerns or fears do you have?
- What aspects of the trip do you think will be the hardest for you?
- What specialized skills do you think are needed for a mission trip?
- What will you need help with on the mission trip?

The covenant the group builds can be expressed in a contract format using the Trip Expectations and Rules resource on page 95. This sample contract states clear expectations of each participant. Requiring everyone to complete and sign a statement of commitment formalizes their intention and responsibility to be a fully participating group member. Anyone who cannot complete this step in a timely manner may not be a candidate for the level of commitment and rigor that mission trips require.

A covenant generated by the group provides security for youth and adults alike while on the trip. Having each participant carry a copy of the contract can help bind the group's commitment. Since the contract captures a point in time, the group can draft a new version that includes other elements that arise out of the advance group process. In addition to the expectations listed above, others might include:

- Show up for scheduled group check-in time.
- Bring your whole self, with reverence.
- Use "I" statements.
- Respect confidentiality.
- Pay attention to make sure there is balance in sharing; try not to speak too much or too little.
- Ride out feelings of discomfort or ask for help.
- Don't quit—ask for a break.
- Follow safety precautions.

Devoting time to a daily check-in should be a central piece of the covenant. Because each person processes new experiences differently, some may resist the idea of participating in this intimate time. A healthy group should be prepared to commit to this important covenantal system to bear witness to each other's struggles, insights, questions, and growth. Waiting until the trip to establish how and when to do a daily check-in is too late, since all the participants' energy will be focused on adapting to the new environment.

Trip Expectations and Rules

Since it is not possible to create a set of rules that could address every scenario of the mission trip, it is important to create an absolute expectation that all youth participants will respect and adhere to the leadership of the adult trip advisors. Although many parents and caretakers believe their youth are empowered to make their own decisions, they must also acknowledge the trial-and-error learning process of youth. A mission trip is not the place to test limits. Give utmost importance to the needs and logistics of managing a group, not individuals. If a youth or adult does not understand or agree with the trip expectations, the issue should be addressed prior to the departure date. During the trip, adult advisors will need compliance from the whole team to keep each and all participants safe and on task. The trip is not the time to sort out differences of opinion that are unrelated to the completion of the mission.

Participating in a mission trip will provide the opportunity to view the world through a different lens and help you understand some ways to put your Unitarian Universalist faith into action and make a difference in the world. Even before you get on the plane, you will feel like part of a great team that has worked together for a common goal. With each other's support, you will likely feel that your "search for truth and meaning" is making the questions bigger and the call to action stronger. While not impossible, such an experience is often difficult to have at home, in familiar surroundings, where you must deal with the responsibilities of daily routines. One of the most surprising and profound aspects of a mission trip is the joy of being part of a larger experience, one you share with friends you make in just a couple of days. Just a few days of working, playing, and laughing with friendly local children and youth will change you forever.

The general list of rules and expectations are:

- Do not bring anything that is not on the packing list without prior approval.
- Local cultural expectations of dress and behavior will be followed and doctrine/mission of site staff will be respected. (Note: Use discretion in bringing T-shirts with writing on them.)
- Be polite and respectful.
- Always clean up after yourselves.
- Take initiative during this trip by noticing or asking what needs to be done; it will not be the responsibility of the adults to direct youth.
- No leaving the group at any time.
- No weapons of any kind.
- Drugs, drinking, and smoking are not permitted.
- No disobedience to a trip advisor or site foreperson.
- Differences of opinions should be addressed respectfully and directly.
- No swearing, offensive language, or cultural slurs.
- No sexualized behavior and no exclusive behavior (cliques).
- All youth must be willing to comply with team leadership.

Please note that if anyone violates any of the mission trip rules and expectations, parent(s) will be informed immediately. A violation may result in a one-way ticket back home at your own expense. Participation in this trip indicates your agreement with adult team leadership to follow these rules.

The mission trip advisors are available to discuss rules and expectations in advance of the trip.

I've read the above and agree to all the expectations.

Youth Signature ______________________________________

Parent Signature ______________________________________

Resource

Team-Building Games

Some of the most powerful group activities involve members playing games that reveal group dynamics, personality qualities, and a fresher understanding of interpersonal relations. There is a wide variety of team-building games and activities, with excellent resources in print and online. The resources in this section are a good place to start.

Deep Fun is a complete resource compiled by the Unitarian Universalist Association. It provides many games, from simple to complex, arranged by stages of community building. Explore these stages by reading the resource that begins on page 99, "Five Steps of Community Building." This essay, widely used in Unitarian Universalist youth programming, will help you understand the stages of your team's development so you can choose the most useful game or activity. Download *Deep Fun* at no charge from www.uua.org/leaders/leaderslibrary/deepfun/index.shtml

Taking any type of personality test as a group can accelerate relationship building and team identity. The intended outcome is simply a greater understanding of how our characteristics and traits affect our ability to communicate and interact. Youth of all learning styles will find it easy to comprehend a simplified version of any personality test. One of the best tests for youth is in Sean Covey's book *The 7 Habits of Highly Effective Teens.* Covey uses fruit names to describe four main personality types.

Two additional online sources, SALTO-YOUTH Resource Centres and Ultimate Camp Resource, provide quick-access resources. SALTO (Support, Advanced Learning and Training Opportunities)

is a European resource network for youth programs that provides a free, easy-to-use game and activity training database (www.salto-youth.net). Ultimate Camp Resource is an online community and website that offers extensive, free resources for group activities, sorted into categories, including art projects, games, skits, songs, stories, icebreakers, and team builders. Although the activities are designed for use at camps, you will find that your team can use many as they are or easily adapt them (www.ultimatecamp resource.com).

Five Steps of Community Building

Adapted by Jennifer Martin and Galen Moore from "Building Community in Youth Groups" by Denny Rydberg.

Step One: Bonding

The first step in building community is to break down the cliques and barriers that exist, and to establish a relationship of trust among the individuals in the group. A problem-solving task or other activity that requires group members to work side by side can create communal bonds. As they discuss solutions and help one another accomplish the goal, group members transcend their diverse backgrounds. Cooperation is the goal. As each person's input is accepted and welcomed by others, they begin to identify as part of the team.

Step Two: Opening Up

When an individual can share non-threatening areas of their life, an exciting step in group building has taken place. If one person perceives that another is genuinely interested in their story, then trust will develop between the two. Unfortunately, the reverse is also true. If a person perceives that others do not care enough to listen, trust—the foundation of community—will not be established. The more sympathetically a group listens, the more secure an individual feels as a member of a group.

The exercises you do in this step should be flexible, so that people can share to whatever degree they feel comfortable. Participants go away from these activities enthusiastic about the deepening friendships they are developing in their group. They realize that their personal imperfections and struggles are shared by the group. Individuals discover that their uniqueness is not strange but wonderful, and the group accepts and loves them.

Step Three: Affirming

The act of encouraging each other through affirmation is crucial to the growing process of a group. When a young man's peers compliment him, he feels more confident in himself in relation to the group and can share deeper feelings. When friends tell a young woman that they appreciate her, she realizes that she is worthy of love and praise. Many reclusive youth become active members of the group when they realize others care about them. Participants in affirming interactions leave feeling warm and fuzzy about the group and themselves. This feeling is especially crucial at this stage of the community-building process. After Step Two, Opening Up, people need positive feedback before they will consider sharing further. Remember that adult leaders and advisors are an integral part of the community-building process and need affirmation just like everyone else.

Step Four: Stretching

Difficult situations naturally arise if the group is together long enough. These include problems that arise in group members' lives, like divorce, illness, and drug abuse, or those that affect the group directly, like division of the church, rules violation, and cliques at conferences. These situations are opportunities for stretching. However, since many youth groups are together for only a short period, you may not want to wait for a stretching experience to surface on its own. It is sometimes necessary to initiate one.

Stretching exercises reap many benefits. When people move beyond their normal comfort level, they experience the greatest potential for growth. Group members facing struggles together must actively care for each other. Individuals cannot merely say they care for each other in a stretching exercise; they must actively show it. They must create an atmosphere in which people feel comfortable enough to expose their imperfections to the group. For example, if the group plans a trip to the hospital to visit terminally ill children, a popular member who appears to have his life together might admit his apprehensions about talking one-on-one with those less fortunate than he. When he sees that the group still likes him, he realizes that his facade of perfection is unnecessary. And when self-critical members of the group discover that even seemingly perfect people have struggles, they will be less hard on themselves.

Through a simple stretching exercise, individuals also realize they can achieve much more as a group than they could as a collection of individuals. They realize the importance of each member to the entire group. Facing and overcoming programmed difficulties give young people the confidence to cope with the everyday problems they face. They learn that they can accomplish more than they thought possible, if they believe in themselves.

Step Five: Deeper Sharing and Goal Setting

At this stage, individuals share deeply with one another and set goals. The youth group becomes a setting where young people can express their visions of the future and present struggles. The group will not laugh at or condemn its members if they admit they flunked a test, or that they dream of becoming a U.S. senator, or that they have a drinking problem.

When a group member shares a problem, the rest of the group gives support and encouragement by expressing sympathy. The group can help the individual talk through possible solutions and goals. The group holds the individual accountable for his or her decisions, remaining supportive throughout the process.

Keep in mind that not all of a person's thoughts are appropriate to share in a group setting. A person should be discouraged from telling the entire youth group details of her life that might hurt another member of the group. She should be encouraged to share these struggles with only one other or the advisor(s) on a one-to-one basis and, in these conversations, come up with a suitable way to bring it to the group.

Action

Taking a group through the five steps is essential to a communal group, but it is only the beginning of the exercises' benefits. Once they have built a sense of community, participants will be ready to risk sharing with their peers in a non-programmed way. They will also be ready to set and accomplish other goals with a united effort.

Accessibilities and Comfort Levels

There is one crucial element in community building: making sure you are including everyone. One part that is often overlooked is that not everyone's comfort level or physical abilities are the same. For example, not everyone has the same level of comfort around touch, personal sharing, or personal space. Likewise, many people have varying levels of ability to engage in physical activities. Some differing abilities are quite noticeable, like being in a wheelchair or using some implement to assist with mobility. Others might not be as easy to see, such as sight or hearing impairments or back trouble that makes sitting on the floor difficult or uncomfortable. The following helpful hints will ensure that your community-building activities include everyone.

Know your audience

It is always a good idea to come into an activity with a couple of program ideas in mind, so that if you have to make changes on the fly, you can. Observe your audience to see if there are any obvious impediments to the activity you have planned. Always explain the activity and then ask if anyone might have a problem participating.

Know what's appropriate

Many activities involve the kinds of physical contact or discussion/sharing that are okay when it's youth-with-youth or adult-with-adult, but not appropriate for youth-with-adult. Adults should be aware of those situations and either sit out or pair with other adults as appropriate. Youth should respect an adult's decision to pass.

It is always OK to pass

Make it clear that any participant can pass at any time during the activities. If you are doing an intense activity, also make sure that a chaplain or other qualified adult is available to help a participant process the experience.

Modify! Modify! Modify!

If someone cannot take part in an activity, for whatever reason, ask them how the activity might be modified so they could take part.

Spiritual Preparation

If you have accepted the premise of this guidebook—that undertaking a mission trip is a transformative experience in developing one's faith as a Unitarian Universalist—then how your group prepares spiritually for the mission trip is as vital as making sure they packed their suitcases with everything they need. Each mission trip is unique, so each will provide a variety of opportunities for religious and spiritual exploration. The main point is to be intentional about including a spiritual component throughout your experience. Each phase calls for a different approach.

Before the Trip

Here are some questions to consider during regular monthly meetings (or more frequently, if desired).

How will we gather?
Honor the spiritual significance of the group undertaking this journey together. Start each meeting by lighting a chalice, sharing a short, themed reading, and posing a question for reflection.

How will we build connections within the group?
The work that is done in team building creates the necessary comfort, trust, and intimacy within the group, and also serves as an investment for the trip itself when the group calls upon those bonds.

Whom are we serving?
How will you learn about the people with whom you will be working? What books can you read to learn about the people, their culture, their faith, and the political climate, to help you understand the social injustice they are experiencing?

How does Unitarian Universalism inform our experience?
Explore ways in which the mission trip is an expression of both individual and collective (group) Unitarian Universalist faith. Think about UU Principles, the Sources of the UU living tradition, or participants' personal credos. How do they inform the work? Learn about other Unitarian Universalists who have a history of involvement in this or similar work. Learn about possible theological significance and connections.

How will we respect and honor the different faiths and personal spiritual paths of others?
The faith of people in the community where you will be working may differ from what is familiar to your group. What information about the spiritual/religious beliefs or practices of the people you will be serving and the organization with which you will be working is valuable for your group to learn? How will you learn about your faith as a Unitarian Universalist if you are working with people from another faith tradition? How will you demonstrate competence in respecting another culture and faith tradition and avoid misappropriation?

How will we prepare for a difficult or challenging experience?
Consider creating a ritual prior to your departure to dedicate your group and honor the willingness of the group to undertake this experience together. Offer participants the opportunity to give voice to the things they are excited about or look forward to, as well as the things they are nervous about or fear. Acknowledge that there probably will be both moments of joy and fun and moments of sadness and challenge along the way. It is difficult to know

exactly how to prepare for a trip like this, and some of the trepidation people are feeling, if any, may be due to the unknown. Explain that approaching the mission trip with an open mind and heart and a willingness to serve establishes the spiritual framework for the journey to begin. Inform the group of the ways you anticipate being able to process or reflect on your experiences during the trip itself.

During the Trip

Framing each day with intentional checkpoints and activities is essential to nurturing group dynamics and deepening the experience. While the purpose of each day may be defined by hands-on work, the group covenant keeps the vision firmly in place. Sometimes the work requires the group to disperse to different locations or the group leaders may not be in direct control of time management. In spite of these potential difficulties, prioritizing group activities is a key planning issue. As you review your trip schedule with the host organization, make explicit your intention to allocate time for group activities that maintain the spiritual context for the work.

Power circles

There will be times that you need to assemble the group quickly. These include when you start and end the day, re-gather smaller teams, and take energy and meal breaks. Establish a catch phrase, such as "Power circle!" that lets the group know it is time to gather around the speaker.

Spirit circles

A longer, end-of-day check-in time is as important as beginning the day in an intentional way—perhaps more. Spirit circles will provide time, grounding, and space for sharing the highs and lows of your trip. It will also offer opportunities for participants to process what they are experiencing. Gather the group, light a chalice, share a reading, and check in with one another. This is an especially effective way to observe how people are faring physically, emotionally, and spiritually and gauge the temperature of the group.

Spirit circles provide a safe place where participants can express intense emotions—evidence that they are processing the experience at an authentic level. In the spirit circle, participants' responses or behavior can also indicate whether they are having trouble. The group leader or another adult on the trip must have the skills to recognize and address the need for individual pastoral support, apart from the group. This is an essential requirement. Find detailed guidance for planning and leading power circles and spirit circles in the Ritual and Worship section on page 111.)

Journaling

Consider providing all team members with a journal before you leave home. A simple notebook or composition book will do. (You might also consider having youth decorate and personalize their journals during a group activity before the trip.) Encourage people to journal about their experiences on a daily basis and provide dedicated time to do so. Journaling is an especially effective tool for supporting participants as they process their feelings individually, rather than in the context of the group, and may be more comfortable for some people.

In addition, journaling provides participants with a commentary on their experience. This is especially useful when preparing a worship service after you return from the trip. While there is no "right" way to journal, it helps to provide prompts for those who would welcome having an entry point for their reflection. For more suggestions, see the Journaling resource on page 115.

Prayer

Coming face-to-face with injustice and suffering is rarely, if ever, easy. Often, knowing how to respond is a challenge. Prayer provides us with a way to center ourselves and engage in sacred dialogue.

Worship on site

Attending worship in the community can be an act of solidarity with the people you are supporting. It also can provide an opportunity to learn more about the local culture. Some team members will experience a local community worship service as an occasion for spiritual reflection and renewal. Whatever their motivation for attending worship, participants should be mindful, prepared, respectful guests in the community's worship setting.

Providing opportunities for participants to create their own worship is another effective way for the group to reflect on and express the spiritual significance of their experience. Creating worship can be as simple as having some group members plan and lead a spirit circle for the group.

Spiritual preparation for returning home

For many, the processing will continue and the significance will resonate long after returning home from a mission trip. While on the trip, help participants plan for returning to the rhythms of their daily lives. Telling them what to expect when they arrive home does some measure of good and is an adequate starting point. See Chapter 7, "Unpacking Your Bags," on page 41, for a detailed discussion of how the return can unfold and how leaders can facilitate team members' positive and fruitful adjustment.

After the Trip

The mission trip can be a spark that leads to a long-term commitment to building a just and peaceful world. Plan tangible ways for participants to continue their reflection on the experience and share their learning with others. Foster the connections they have made with one another. Encourage the group to extend the mission by continuing social justice work together. Attend to the spiritual content of all post-trip gatherings to support participants' deepest growth and transformation.

Mission trip reunion

Because of the close personal relationships that developed during the trip, the team will want and need to reconnect shortly after they return. Re-entering everyday life can be challenging, so scheduling a time to support each other's process is important. The group will also need to follow up with actions such as writing thank-you notes or exchanging items they have borrowed from one another. Gatherings immediately after the trip can involve the team only, include their families, too, or take the form of a potluck at the congregation or at someone's home. The important piece is to bring the group together and celebrate.

Worship

After such a milestone experience, it is time to bring the mission home into the congregational worship setting. Marrying some expression of the group's experience with the congregation's practice and liturgy integrates the mission trip into the living ministry of the congregation. The group's contribution to worship might share some of the youths' wrestling with big questions that emerged during the trip, explore the trip's effect on their developing faith and Unitarian Universalist identity, or issue a spiritually grounded call to action.

Forum

A stand-alone program featuring a travelogue presentation about the day-to-day occurrences of the trip is informative and will likely be appreciated by parents, supporters, and future participants.

Audio/slide/video show

An audiovisual presentation is an appealing and effective way to share information and stories about the mission trip with the congregation. Your group can create a presentation to include in worship, at a forum, on the congregation's website, or simply as a display at coffee hour.

Passing the torch

Schedule opportunities for team members to serve as ambassadors to others interested in similar or related mission work. While cultivating leaders among the youth, you will also help keep the spirit and learning of the mission trip alive and potentially spark more enthusiasm and transform it into social justice ministry.

What's Next?

New and close relationships among the trip participants and the congregation's enthusiastic welcome home make this the time to build on the positive gains of the mission. Discuss ways the mission trip can be integrated into and inform the social justice ministry of the congregation. Explore connections of all kinds, such as partnerships with other youth groups, interfaith service groups, and other communities. Find out how your mission fits with other initiatives and organizations in your community. Use generative questions such as these:

- What local connections can and should we make in our community?
- What are people already doing to serve this need?
- Who in the congregation is interested in working toward the goals we are now engaged in?
- Who is directly involved in community initiatives relevant to our focus?
- How can other youth and younger children in our congregation become connected to their peers whom we met but whom they did not meet directly?

Ritual and Worship

Any worship that is not a fixed, regular Sunday morning service is usually considered “alternative.” With this descriptor comes a world of possibilities for creating sacred space wherever you are. On a mission trip, you might use a power circle each morning and a spirit circle to close each day.

Charge the Day with a Power Circle

A structured gathering can set the tone for any day or for a task you will do together. Whether the entire group gathers before heading to a worksite or you call a “team circle” to energize a smaller working group, you can create a power circle using a variety of elements, such as gathering questions, music, games, and structured assignments for increasing your awareness during the course of the day

Gathering questions

Gathering questions are prompts to bring the group to a common focus. Encourage everyone to listen as each participant briefly reflects on the same question. Of course, participants may pass. Sample questions include:

- What are your goals or hopes for this day?
- How will you know when you have reached your goals for this day?
- What do you think will be the hardest part of today?
- What song is playing in your head right now?

- What one word describes how you are feeling right now?
- Name your "high/low" from yesterday—the high point, or most joyful moment, for you or the most challenging, or sad, moment for you.

Music
A musician in your group or a willing song leader can lead a quick round everyone knows, to energize the gathering.

Riddles or games
Read a few selections from a book of riddles or lead a game from *Deep Fun*, a resource in the online Leaders Library of the UUA website, www.uua.org. Give the group a quick way to interact and problem solve in a light-hearted way as a break from the mission work of the day. See Team-Building Games on page 97 for additional suggestions.

Assignment for the day: Noticing
Prompt the group to notice sensory details throughout the day, to encourage them to pay attention to more than what is directly in front of them. Give a specific assignment during the morning power circle, and ask for a check-in during the end-of-the-day spirit circle. Some suggestions are:

- Look for the most surprisingly creative solution of the day.
- What color jumps out to you?
- What do you smell? What does it remind you of?
- Name something you have seen or experienced today for the very first time.
- Close your eyes and take note of what you hear.
- Keep track of the animals you see in one day. Name the ones you remember.
- Pick a moment during the day and "take a picture" by writing a haiku about it.
- See how many new things you can try today.

If the team has a camera, you might assign a participant to document each day. Invite youth to ask local children to show them their favorite things or places, or their family and friends, and take pictures. If you have an instant camera, take two photos—one for the mission team, the other for local residents. If possible, arrange to send prints of the photographs to the people at the mission site after your team arrives home. Remind participants to always seek permission from residents before taking photographs.

Spirit Circles: Closing the Day with Sharing and Reflection

No matter how busy or tiring the day has been, a contemplative group check-in is essential to the well-being and caretaking of the group. Participants will come to appreciate time to sit in a space that allows them to consider their day's encounters in a deeper way. At times, folks who are having a very powerful, perhaps uncomfortable experience find support and understanding in the circle of sharing and caring. In some cases, the discomfort can cause a person to retreat from the group. However, with a solid covenant in place that includes showing up for daily check-in and offering and accepting help, the spirit circle can encourage engagement with difficult feelings rather than retreat.

In other words, it is not advisable to make this time optional for any team member. Our covenantal relationships call for a commitment to show up for each other unconditionally.

Some of the elements and prompts in the spirit circle might be the same as the morning power circle. However, the tenor of this circle should be contemplative, rather than energizing. Follow up on a prompting question that was offered in the morning or introduce other, more challenging or serious questions for group sharing in the spirit circle. These could include:

- What differences do you see between your own life at home and the way people live where you are serving?
- What parts of the lifestyle in this new environment are familiar to you?

- How do family members interact with each other?
- How do children play?
- Describe an image of joy.
- Describe an image of injustice.
- Describe how the experience of today may have shifted a perception or an assumption you have held.

Whether you dedicate fifteen minutes or an hour to the spirit circle, your group will have a stronger experience if you close each day with intentional time together and a few planned worship elements.

Journaling

Throughout time, people have kept diaries and journals to document significant events, acknowledge the ordinary, keep track of milestones, and process feelings, thoughts, and experiences. There are as many different types of journals (such as baby books, diaries, garden journals, runner's logs, etc.) as there are reasons for keeping them. For the purpose of a mission trip, a journal can be thought of as a travel log—a place for participants to record their thoughts as well as the details of the places, people, and events of the trip.

For those who have never journaled (and as a reminder to those who have), keep in mind that journaling, in its simplest form, is nothing more than a conversation with yourself. There is no intended end product. No one is meant to ever read what you write. So it doesn't matter what you write or how (no one will be looking over your shoulder to correct punctuation or grammar!) It only matters that you try to put on paper what's in your heart and mind.

One approach to journaling is for a leader to offer one or two journal prompts each time the group gathers, based on the particular experience or tone of the day. For example, after a chalice lighting, group check-in, and sharing, give one powerful journal prompt with the expectation of 10–15 minutes of contemplation and writing in silence together. This is an excellent way to strengthen the group's identity and add depth to its shared experience.

Listed below are a number of possible prompts. Several could be given more than once. Afterward, team members may enjoy seeing how they responded differently to the same prompt at different stages of the journey.

Before the Trip

- What are your expectations?
- What gifts do you bring to the work you will be doing?
- What are your dreams for the people you will be serving?
- Write about your spirituality at the age of 7, 14, 21, 28, 35, 42, 49, etc. How has it/will it change?

During the Trip

- What will you take with you from this experience?
- What will you leave behind?
- What have you discovered that surprises you?
- Identify a problem you experienced this week. Now think of a quality you'd need more of in order to solve the problem or meet the challenge (think of a character quality instead of something external, like money). Write down a few, choose one, and write for ten minutes about what it would be like if you had more of this quality (for example, With more patience, I could . . . .).
- Draw your feelings about your experience.
- Describe your ideal community. What examples of this type of community have you witnessed during this trip?
- List the five most astonishing/wonderful/terrible things you have seen or experienced today.
- Where did you encounter the sacred or the holy today (or this week)?
- At the beginning of the day, jot down what you hope to get out of the day. At the day's end, write down what you got.

After the Trip

- Write a letter to someone (perhaps a religious or political leader) about your experience.
- What do you want to do next, now that you've had this mission experience?
- In one word, how would describe your experience? What other experiences in your life would that word describe?

With journaling firmly in place as a spiritual practice, a youth will forever have something to hold onto that marks their amazing journey. And the journals can be a useful reference if the group creates a worship service to share with the congregation, or if individuals later wish to write about their experiences.

Sample Spirit Circle—at Home

Use this spirit circle at a planning meeting before the mission trip or when the group gathers after returning home.

Supplies/Setup

- blanket or chairs in a circle
- chalice, candle, and lighter/extinguisher or an LED/battery-operated candle
- individual candles
- basket
- plenty of scrap paper of all sizes
- pen and ink (available at craft supply)
- pens
- recorded music and music player
  —Gathering music: "Silence," by Delirium
  —Ritual music: "The Slow Wait," by the American Dollar or other meditation music, such as that found on the website Stresslesser.com

Chalice Lighting and Reading

Play the gathering music, "Silence," by Delirium. Invite participants to gather in a circle, with an unlit candle before them. Light the chalice. Say:

> The wise teacher Bodhidharma said that Zen Buddhism is "a special transmission outside the scriptures with no dependence upon words and letters, a direct pointing to the human mind and seeing into one's own nature."

Welcome
Pause for a moment. Then say:

> Our spirit circle today comes from Buddhist Chinese and Japanese traditions. We use the wisdom from Bodhidharma and Buddhist teachings to open up pathways to our human mind to discover our own nature. We know that as Unitarian Universalists, we always have the sacred resources of our Sources to guide us on our journey and give clarity to our beliefs, faith, and right action. It is also part of being Unitarian Universalist to live with big, unspoken questions about our existence and the universe. We know it takes time and a caring community to live into knowing the answers.

Ritual Activity
Introduce the activity by saying:

> As a symbol, the circle represents the wholeness of our being. *Ensō* is a Japanese word meaning "circle." In Zen Buddhism, the *ensō* is the most common subject of art and calligraphy. It symbolizes enlightenment, strength, elegance, the universe, and the void. Although its form is quite simple, the *ensō* is difficult to define. In one way, it is just a circle painted in one brushstroke and a single breath. At the same time, it represents the totality of the great void. The shape can be perfect and symmetrical. The shape can also be irregular. The line can be thin, or it can be broad and thick.
>
> To practice *ensō* we paint circle after circle, either as a way to empty the mind or with one thing in mind. One brushstroke, one breath. While we listen to some music, try some *ensō*, try many. Use as many pieces of paper as you want.

Distribute pens and paper. Play instrumental, tranquil music, such as "The Slow Wait," by the American Dollar. Give the group some time to draw.

Meditation/Silence

Place the empty basket near the lit chalice. Distribute candles and ask participants to place the candles on the ground or floor in front of them. Say:

> What is burning on your mind? What is the biggest question you can feel the weight of inside of you? What do you wonder about deep in your heart that you know might take a long time to answer?

Allow some silence. Then say:

> What question emerged for you in the silence? Write this question down. We'll put the questions in a basket. We will speak them aloud shortly. We will not read our own question. Instead, we will listen to each other speak the words that are our own. Take a moment to write down a big question. When you are done, place the question in the basket and light the candle that is in front of you. Let the candle illuminate your space.

Sharing

When all the candles are lit, say:

> As you are moved, you are invited to take a question. Hold it in your hand and feel the weight, feel the honor. Read the question over several times. With love and deep respect, read the question aloud. Be sure to speak clearly and loud enough so that the question is heard and honored. After you read the question, move your candle to the center of our circle. Let this sacred circle of light emerge before us as the place that holds our big questions, our wonderings, our uncertainties.

Writing Meditation
When the participants have finished, say:

> Now we'll do another Japanese spiritual practice: haiku. Haiku poetry consists of three simple lines. The first line is five syllables, the second line is seven syllables, and the third line is five syllables. Let your own burning question come to mind again. Find a way to ask the question in the form of haiku. Take your time. When you are ready, write your haiku on one of the *ensōs* you created.

Closing Words
Share these words from Rainer Maria Rilke (*Letters to a Young Poet*, 1903):

> Don't search for answers, which could not be given to you now, because you would not be able to live them. And the point is to live everything. Live the questions now. Perhaps then, someday far in the future, you will gradually, without even noticing it, live your way into the answer.

Extinguish the chalice.

Sample Spirit Circle—On the Trip

Use this spirit circle while the group is on the mission trip. If someone in the group can lead a song or accompany on guitar or another instrument, ask them in advance.

Supplies/Setup

- blanket or chairs in a circle
- chalice, candle, and lighter/extinguisher or an LED/battery-operated candle
- pens and journals
- optional: guitar or other instrument and song lyrics
- recorded music and music player
  —Gathering music: "Come, Come, Whoever You Are" #188, *Singing the Living Tradition*
  —Journaling music: "Shape of My Heart," by Sting

Chalice Lighting and Reading

Invite participants to gather in a circle. Share this quotation from South Asian scholar Shefali Milczarek-Desai:

> Some days I wonder if anyone sees that I am all of these at once, and other days it doesn't matter what anyone sees because I am comfortable being a contrary, existing at the margins of categories.

Sing "Come, Come, Whoever You Are." Light the chalice.

Welcome
Pause for moment. Then say:

> We've traveled many miles. For what? To help others? Yes. To make a difference? Yes. To have fun together and get closer? Yes. How many of us came all this way to get to know ourselves better? How many of you want to know YOU better?

Main Idea: Who Am I?
Introduce the theme by saying:

> When you look in the mirror, what do you see? Or rather, who do you see? I don't mean what color your eyes are, whether you need a haircut or a shave, or whether you like your new earrings. I mean *who* do you see? Who are you?
>
> Much of our sense of who we are comes from what people tell us. They tell us in many ways. The way they act around us, the way they treat us, what they say to us. What people think of us has a big impact on our sense of identity, whether we like it or not. So let's consider how we might ask ourselves, "Who am I?" We could start with the question, "Who does everyone think I am?" Consider that for a moment.

Pause. Then say:

> People tell us all the time to "be yourself," "be strong," "believe in yourself." That is really important. Can we do that alone? Doesn't it matter what people think of us? Let's look at that.
>
> I invite you to close your eyes. In this space of meditation, invite all the people who are important to you into your mind space—friends, siblings, parents, teachers, mentors, relatives, role models—invite all of them in. I hope that you are smiling at each other. Now, for a mo-

> ment, in this quiet space, listen to what they are saying to you. Listen only to the positive things they are saying to you. Let that conversation run for a moment. When we come back, we'll use our journals to record some of the conversation we have heard. You can invite in your closest supporters now. Listen to them.

Journal Prompt 1
Allow some silence. Then say:

> Take your journal and pen. What did you hear? Write it down. Write it all down. We'll do that for the next two minutes.

Watch the time, and tell the group when it is up. Then say:

> What do you think? Did you like what you heard? Sometimes the people closest to us are the ones who have the biggest impact on our ability to live into our full potential. Quite often, these well-meaning people do not know you as well as you know you. So you feel there is something missing. Look at what you've written. Look hard. Add anything that you think your people forgot to say to you. Look at what you've written. What do you need to cross out because even though they mean well, that's not really who you are or want to be?

Journal Prompt 2
Describe the second exercise by saying:

> Now you are invited to consider sharing a small vision. If you could pick three words that all your people used to describe you, what would they be? What three words could sum up your sense of self, your identity, your self-worth?
>
> If you had to describe yourself to someone you didn't know, what would you say about yourself? Think for a

> moment. As the spirit moves you, write down these three words. Try writing them different ways—doodle them, write them small, write them in fancy lettering.
>
> After you've written and played with your three words, write them one last time, but write them this way: Before each word, add "I am . . . . " You will have three full sentences. After you write each of the sentences, put an exclamation point at the end of each. Take a look. How does that make you feel?

Play the journaling music, "Shape of My Heart," by Sting. Allow time to write.

Affirmation
Invite sharing by saying:

> Affirmations, sincere ones, feel good. We shouldn't forget to give them to ourselves. But now, consider the work we have done today and consider how we got the work done.

Invite a volunteer to start this sharing by giving an affirmation to the person to their left. Ask them to affirm a way that person contributed to the accomplishments and/or experience of the day. Then, the affirmations can continue, one at a time, around the circle. Tell the group each person is expected to share, so everyone can be affirmed.

Closing Words
Share these words by poet Rabindranath Tagore:

> I slept and dreamt that life was joy,
> I awoke and saw that life was service
> I acted and behold, service was joy.

Extinguish the chalice.